Leading Learning and Together

This is a practical guide for school leaders who want to understand more about how to connect teaching and learning with wellbeing in their school.

This book reimagines school leadership beyond roles and networks and explores new practical possibilities for leading pedagogy. The emphasis is on knowing students and how they learn and supporting leaders to create sustainable, productive learning environments where wellbeing and learning are integral. The book brings theory and practice together through case studies from work in schools, linking the 'Why?' with the 'How', and makes authentic connections between leading pedagogy and wellbeing through practical strategies and clear principles. Further, the book addresses issues of workload and leadership succession through collective job design, with the aim of improving psychosocial safety for all students and school staff.

Drawing on the authors' experience in school leadership and clinical and organisational psychology, this book is designed for school leadership teams looking to work cohesively together while prioritising wellbeing. It will also be relevant to postgraduate studies in educational leadership.

Christine Grice is a Senior Lecturer in educational leadership at The University of Sydney.

Fiona Davies is a Clinical and Organisational Psychologist who has worked in leadership positions in organisational development, in implementation research and as a Clinical Psychologist.

Leading Learning and Wellbeing Together

Getting Started with What Matters in Your School

Christine Grice and Fiona Davies

Routledge
Taylor & Francis Group
LONDON AND NEW YORK

Designed cover image: Getty Images

First published 2026
by Routledge
4 Park Square, Milton Park, Abingdon, Oxon OX14 4RN

and by Routledge
605 Third Avenue, New York, NY 10158

Routledge is an imprint of the Taylor & Francis Group, an informa business

© 2026 Christine Grice and Fiona Davies

The right of Christine Grice and Fiona Davies to be identified as authors of this work has been asserted in accordance with sections 77 and 78 of the Copyright, Designs and Patents Act 1988.

All rights reserved. No part of this book may be reprinted or reproduced or utilised in any form or by any electronic, mechanical, or other means, now known or hereafter invented, including photocopying and recording, or in any information storage or retrieval system, without permission in writing from the publishers.

Trademark notice: Product or corporate names may be trademarks or registered trademarks, and are used only for identification and explanation without intent to infringe.

British Library Cataloguing-in-Publication Data
A catalogue record for this book is available from the British Library

ISBN: 978-1-032-93196-8 (hbk)
ISBN: 978-1-032-93195-1 (pbk)
ISBN: 978-1-003-56484-3 (ebk)

DOI: 10.4324/9781003564843

Typeset in Galliard
by SPi Technologies India Pvt Ltd (Straive)

Contents

List of Figures ix
List of Contributors x
Preface xi
Acknowledgements xii

Introduction: Pedagogy: Leading Learning and
Wellbeing in Schools 1

The Whole Child, the Whole Educator, and the Whole School 2
Pedagogy 3
Wellbeing 4
Leading Together 5
Communities are About Relationships 6
Arrangements 7
Who are We? 9
Practice Menu: Leading Learning and Wellbeing Together 12
Summary of Key Points 13
Questions 13
Conclusion 13
Synopsis 14
References 15

1 Understanding the Context of Your School 16

Examples from Schools 16
  Tumult School 17
  Primed School 18
  Eager School 19
Connecting Research and Practice 19
  The Theory of Practice Architectures 21

Leading, Not Leadership 22
Research–Practice Partnerships 23
Leading in Practice 25
  Task 1: Metaphor Task 25
  Task 2: The Middle Leadership Framework 25
  Task 3: Lolly/Sweets/Candy Task: What Does Leadership
    Look Like In Your School? 25
Practice Menu 26
References 28

2   Knowing Yourself and Others   30

Examples from Schools 30
  Self-awareness and Shared Awareness 30
  Leading Pedagogy 32
  Gifts 32
Connecting Research and Practice 34
  Self-Awareness 34
  Pedagogical Gifts 37
  Leading Pedagogy 39
Practice Menu 41
References 43

3   What is Wellbeing and What Can You Do to Increase It?   45

Examples in Schools 45
Connecting Research and Practice 46
  What is Wellbeing? 47
  What do we Know About Educator Wellbeing? 48
Psychosocial Hazards 49
  The Job Demands-Resources Model 50
Negative Wellbeing Outcomes 51
  Poor Physical and Mental Health 51
  Burnout 51
  Work Engagement 53
  Both Processes can be Occurring at Once 53
  Wellbeing Interventions 54
Leading in Practice 55
  Active Listening 55
  Practice Menu 58
References 59

Contents vii

4 Trust and Psychological Safety   61

  Examples from Schools 61
    Ana Morphosis School: Remodelling a Distorted Image 62
    Fragmentation School: The Broken Mirror 63
    Cheval School: The Reflective Mirror 65
  Connecting Research and Practice 67
    Psychological Safety 67
    Benefits of Psychological Safety 68
  Trust in Schools 70
    Renewal for Strategic Direction: The Problem with Change
      Champions 72
    Communicative Learning Spaces 73
  Leading in Practice 73
  Practice Menu 74
  References 76

5 The Expansive Role of Leaders: What Do You Do,
  What Could We Do?   78

  Examples from Schools 78
  Connecting Research and Practice 80
    Leading and Learning with Others 81
  Leading in Practice 84
    Recovery from Work 84
    Job Crafting 86
  Practice Menu 87
  References 89

6 Mastering the Practices of Leading Together: Collaboration,
  Capability   92

  Examples from Schools 92
  Connecting Research and Practice 96
  Leading in Practice 97
    Active Listening 98
    Meeting Protocols 98
    Project Initiatives 99
    Socratic Questioning 99
  Practice Menu 100
  References 101

7 Leading Together: Solidarity and Purpose from Collective
   Agency and Autonomy   103

   Examples from Schools 103
   Connecting Research and Practice 108
     Self-Determination Theory 108
     Controlled and Autonomous Motivation 109
     Basic Psychological Needs 110
     Self-Determination Theory at Work 110
   Aboriginal Perspectives on Leading 111
     Self Determination and Aboriginal Community Leadership 112
     Culturally Responsive Leadership 113
   Leading in Practice 114
     Culturally Responsive Leadership 114
     Taylorism or Ecologies of Practices 114
     Role Modelling 115
     Autonomy and Collective Agency 116
     Practicing Solidarity of Purpose 116
   Practice Menu 118
   References 119

8 How Will We Get There? Collective Job Crafting   122

   What is Collective Job Crafting? 122
   Examples from Schools 124
   Connecting Research and Practice 128
     Social Network Theory 129
   Leading in Practice 130
     Step 1: Who are We? 130
     Step 2: How do We Work Together? 131
     Step 3: What do We Need? 131
     Step 4: How can We Get There? 132
     Step 5: How are We Going? 133
   Practice Menu 133
   References 135

Index   137

Figures

0.1	Pedagogy and wellbeing spiral	11
1.1	Middle leadership framework	20
8.1	Collective job crafting process	123
8.2	Ecologies of practices for leading together	129

Contributors

Christine Grice

The University of Sydney, Australia

Christine Grice is Postgraduate Coordinator and Senior Lecturer in Educational Leadership at The University of Sydney.

Fiona Davies

The University of Sydney, Australia

Fiona Davies is a Clinical and Organisational Psychologist working with Dr Christine Grice at the University of Sydney.

Tarunna Sebastian

The University of Sydney, Australia

Tarunna Sebastian is a Lecturer in Aboriginal Education at The University of Sydney.

Michelle Donelly

Southern Cross University, Australia

Michelle Donelly is an adjunct associate professor in the Faculty of Health at Southern Cross University, Australia.

Preface

Five years ago, Christine and Fiona were invited into a school to work with leaders on leading pedagogy together through learning and wellbeing. Further invitations came, and we continued working together developing research and professional learning interventions codesigned with school leaders, known as Research–Practice Partnerships. We designed professional learning for middle leaders and a postgraduate unit of study for middle leaders at the University of Sydney. We very quickly became aware of a plethora of professional learning material helping individual leaders. Schools were seeking ways for their leaders to work together in sustainable ways and they were seeking ways of supporting wellbeing and learning. Our book supports school leaders wanting to work together leading pedagogy through learning and wellbeing. We chose to write a book so that we could help more schools, and give back to our participants.

The authors themselves have worked in a range of capacities, and our own research and professional experiences have influenced our writing. Christine has co-led three large Australian research projects for school middle leaders. The patterns and issues that emerged in these projects influenced our book. Christine is an experienced Australian educator, who has worked in a range of teaching and leadership capacities in primary and secondary schools over several decades.

Fiona started her career as an Organisational Psychologist and later trained as a Clinical Psychologist. She has years of experience interviewing hundreds of people at all levels in multiple organisations to understand their experiences at work. She has also worked therapeutically with many people experiencing workplace stress and burnout and has run workshops on workplace wellbeing for many years. Her PhD was part of a large longitudinal study examining student wellbeing in schools. Similarly to Christine, she has also worked as a team member and middle leader and in executive positions. Her experiences as a leader have informed her practices as a team member and vice versa.

Researchers can be siloed in disciplines, and we worked hard to create an interdisciplinary book encompassing ideas from philosophy, sociology, and psychology. By bringing together knowledge and practices from these different fields, we are attempting to bring a hopeful perspective to school improvement which incorporates pedagogical purpose, a systems perspective, and care for the whole person, whether they are an educator or a student.

Acknowledgements

We wish to thank all the Australian school leaders we have worked with over the past five years for their generosity in listening, learning, and sharing their perspectives on leading pedagogy through learning and wellbeing together. You inspired us.

We would also like to thank postgraduate education students at The University of Sydney, who have also shared their own middle leadership experiences with us. Two of our students are cited in this book, with their consent, and we would like to thank Jordan Russo and Kelly Ho for their insightful contributions.

We also wish to thank Tom Batty, from Wildwood Self-Directed Forest School, for inviting us to visit Wildwood and for the opportunity to share his insights into education in our book.

Finally, we would like to thank family, friends and colleagues who generously reviewed chapters for us and provided valuable feedback. This book is dedicated to children and young people and to innovative and to creative people who seek to work together, for their learning and wellbeing.

Introduction
Pedagogy: Leading Learning and Wellbeing in Schools

This chapter is about the whole child, the whole educator, and the whole school. The chapter introduces the authors and helps educators to reflect on their purpose by understanding *What's our why?* in relation to pedagogy, wellbeing, and learning together in community. The emphasis of this book is on doing: on building doinghabits and practices from clear principles of leading pedagogy and wellbeing together. This chapter introduces the context for leading together in schools and invites teachers and school leaders to think about what they see as essential for leading learning and wellbeing in schools today. These principles are derived from our backgrounds in Educational Leadership and Organisational Psychology. We introduce a Pedagogy and Wellbeing Spiral in this chapter to support practice. A menu of practices that has come from our work with schools gives school leaders a focus for discussion in this chapter and in each subsequent chapter, with reflection questions to consider.

Has anyone asked you why you became an educator and what you value most about what you do? As a teacher or a school leader, do you get to do what you value every day? Is there anything that you routinely do that you don't really think teachers should be doing? Is there anything you wish you could spend more time doing?

We invite teachers and school leaders to think about what they see as essential for leading learning and wellbeing in schools today. Additionally, we invite you to consider what pedagogy, leading learning, and wellbeing could mean in schools and how these might relate to what you value most in your specific context. Sometimes what we value is separate from what we do, and this impacts our job satisfaction. Alternatively, sometimes schools ask teachers and leaders to sacrifice their time for *what is good for the school*, with little buy-in. This book is about prioritizing, and then doing together with others, what you think your school values and needs most. Rather than fixing, we focus on connecting people in all practices, for improving leading together, by continually returning to values and purpose.

Leading, pedagogy, and wellbeing are closely intertwined. This book defines leading as a practice that happens between people. We understand that people have individual role titles. We refer to senior leaders who may be deputy

DOI: 10.4324/9781003564843-1

heads, or hold other senior titles in schools, or even the principal. We also include middle leaders who lead teams of teachers whilst teaching classes, as well as talking about teachers. However, this book is less about who you are and more about what you do. It is about understanding more about how you lead together by reflecting on practices that are about *me*, *we*, and *us*.

The original Greek definition of pedagogy means to *lead the child*. Pedagogy encompasses everything schools do for the whole child: their learning and their wellbeing. Teaching techniques and pedagogical approaches might support some aspects of pedagogy, but our definition focuses on the child, not the teacher.

The term, wellbeing, is about the whole child and the whole educator. Our focus is on workplace wellbeing that involves interest and pleasure, meaning and purpose, and minimises distress.

Leading pedagogy through learning and wellbeing are connected practices. The practices that connect with leading pedagogy through learning and wellbeing that we refer to throughout this book are derived from two educational fields: psychology and educational leadership. We seek to connect the practices of leading pedagogy through learning and wellbeing by using a practice spiral that demonstrates what practices are foundational for leading together and what is optimal.

Each chapter provides scenarios from real leaders. We then explain the theory behind each of the examples from schools. A menu of practices at the end of each chapter gives school leaders a focus for discussion. These have come from our work with school leaders. There are reflection questions at the end to consider.

The Whole Child, the Whole Educator, and the Whole School

Schools where students and teachers can flourish are places where people can be authentic. By providing research evidence and lived examples from the experiences of educators, we emphasise the importance of relationships amongst educators and the collective aspects of leading pedagogy and wellbeing. Leading pedagogy and leading educator wellbeing are best considered as parts of a whole rather than as separate entities.

Plenty of professional learning programs and books focus on the individual leader. This book is different because it calls on the whole team to work together. Each chapter will show you how and why working together is the most effective way to lead pedagogy through learning and wellbeing. The team may just start with you (*me*) or your department (*we*), or the work might start with your senior leaders or your middle leaders. Leading together is more challenging to implement, because it takes shared commitment from people. Leading together helps school leaders to live what they value. It is more sustainable. It. The practices throughout the book support teacher and leader wellbeing, and in turn the wellbeing of students, because leading together is designed to tackle the challenges of schooling together.

Pedagogy

Pedagogy is often defined simply as teaching techniques. Teaching techniques are pedagogical *approaches* and are helpful in teaching and learning, but teaching techniques do not get to the heart of pedagogy. Teaching techniques or pedagogical approaches may tempt us to see pedagogy as only a practice that we *do to* children. Even if we think about pedagogical approaches we use *with* children, we may narrow our focus to teaching or to one aspect of learning, which may subtly lead us away from thinking about the child as a whole person, where other people *do* wellbeing for children in the school. If pedagogy invites us to think about leading the child, learning and wellbeing cannot be separated in a person: learning and wellbeing or working and wellbeing are inextricably connected. Pedagogy is always about both. Leading the whole child involves respectfully leading self and others, where teachers and children bring their authentic selves to work and to the classroom. Leading pedagogy is about being self-aware and about teachers and leaders being motivated by their capacity to use their pedagogical gifts with others as a learner and consequently a teacher. In this way, leading pedagogy, or leading the whole child and their learning, is not solo work but a series of together practices or collective practices about *me* and *we* and *us* as learners. A school middle leader reflects on pedagogy:

> Recently I was provoked by the idea that a teacher who is exceedingly proficient in the techniques of classroom instruction does not necessarily make them pedagogically proficient. Even without the professional experience of my colleagues, being part of a school feels natural. I even get joy out of bumping into current and ex-students in the 'real' world – even if they sometimes run in the opposite direction. At first, I thought this was symptomatic of my 'early-career' energy and it would be something that would naturally dissipate over time. Some comments from my colleagues have probably influenced this view. However, I realise that despite lacking time in the game I am a pedagogue in the true sense of the word: a leader of children. I see my role as one that extends beyond the confines of the classroom – even the school gates – where the things I do, I say, and the way I relate to others are part of a much larger, interrelated ecosystem. I feel that siloing learning into subject-specific faculties or leadership domains reduces teaching and learning to instruction; a notion that is far too restrictive for me and my practice. This pedagogical lens also makes sense when I consider my professional identity and personal values. What drew me to education was its liberating quality; a way of preparing young people to face the world with criticality and agency. It is innately democratic. It is fundamentally an act of service. While professional experience is extremely useful, I realise that my capabilities and innate disposition towards understanding the multifaceted, dynamic nature of education is likely why I have come to be in a middle leader position 'quickly'.

Leading the whole child is about respecting self and others, taking responsibility for learning and communicating and ways of working together collectively, serving each other. Leading the child involves understanding that the child can also lead themselves and lead us. Pedagogy is reciprocity in practice.

Wellbeing

Our attitudes to workplace wellbeing are socially and culturally bound. For example, in our own setting in Australia, there is a tendency to see being *"professional"* as divorcing our internal state and private lives from our work and appearing calm and collected. Wellbeing becomes a performance rather than a felt state. We bring our whole selves to work – and this can be of enormous benefit to our work performance and our relationships at work, as we will discuss in this book.

Psychological research on occupational stress and psychological injury has shown for decades that workplace factors affect wellbeing, and yet almost all workplace interventions are focused on individuals. This reflects deeply embedded attitudes that wellbeing is an individual responsibility and that somehow the situation you are in should have no impact on you. Psychologically, this makes no sense at all – we are not islands; we are social people affected by our context. A middle leader shares what workplace wellbeing looks like in their school context:

> Workplace wellbeing is still a relatively new concept in the Vietnamese workplace, and even more so at my international school. Conversations about wellbeing typically focus on students… When it comes to teachers, staff, and school leaders, wellbeing is rarely addressed in a meaningful way, it is simply assumed that everyone is *"healthy"* and *"strong minded"* without any real understanding of our true state…wellbeing initiatives at my school have often focused too heavily on individual-based programs such as one-on-one therapy sessions or resilience workshops while overlooking the harmful work conditions that contribute to stress in the first place.

While there is no doubt that what we bring to work has an impact on our wellbeing, what work brings to us is also important. This is reflected in a growing international focus on psychosocial risks at work as well as increasing research evidence showing the wide range of factors that impact on teacher wellbeing. The impact of teacher and leader wellbeing are a consistent finding in this research and linked to the leading practices we have included in this book.

Wellbeing is complex and defined in many ways. We define it here in terms of three related components. The first is an absence of high levels of ongoing distress (e.g., diagnosed mental health problems or burnout). The second consists of experiences of work that include pleasure and interest. The final component is a sense of meaning and purpose; this is reflected in the words of our middle leader quoted in the pedagogy section above: *"What drew me to education was its liberating quality; a way of preparing young people to face the world with criticality and agency.*" Pedagogy and wellbeing are entwined for this educator in a meaningful and practical way, leading to experiences of "joy" and "energy". They are, in a very real sense, bringing their whole selves to work.

Leading Together

Thinking about leadership usually starts with *me* as an individual and my role or position in the school. One middle leader reflects:

> Next year I am taking on a new position at my school, moving from a wellbeing role to one in teaching and learning. My new responsibilities include developing and implementing a future-focused learning vision that is grounded in creativity, innovation and forward thinking, and providing students with the skills and knowledge to access the world beyond the classroom.

So much of what we do in schools is solo work, whether that be teachers in classrooms, students completing individual tasks, or leaders asserting their individual responsibility, personal vision, or a necessary accountability for a system mandate as principals or even as individual middle leaders or teacher leaders. We bring ourselves to school, and what matters to *me* is important for our personal growth.

Position, role, and responsibility are important for conceptualising leadership and how we are connecting with others in our role, thinking about the ways that *we* work together leading pedagogy through learning and wellbeing:

> Currently my role involves working with the Director of Teaching and Learning and Heads of Departments to design cross-curricular opportunities for students. In the past these opportunities have generally come in the form of projects, assessments, and lesson activities.

We also have those satisfying moments where *we* work together on curriculum change or a school event. These '*we*' moments where we solve problems together and share goals and ideas build trust and collegiality through respect, self-awareness, and awareness of others. In these moments, we are leading together. These moments are about how *we* work together.

Leading together in schools is usually driven by an initiative. It is interesting to reflect on the extent to which the relational dynamic between students and between teachers and leaders is considered, measured, or even valued in schools:

> While the overarching vision for the role fits within a paradigm of lifelong learning, it neglects to conceptualise pedagogy as an all-encompassing practice beyond instruction: the practices that occur in the cultural-discursive and material-economic dimensions are prioritised over those in the social-political dimension. There is a greater focus on what teachers

and students do and say rather than the way they relate to their work and each other. An example of this is that the success of programs, assessments, and resources are measured by the physical products produced – no evaluation tool considers the relational dynamics. This subconsciously promotes an instructional perception of pedagogy that limits opportunities for connectedness and solidarity. The practices that are related to my new role, especially ones that involve staff and students, need to be more considerate of the broader social arrangements within the school. There also needs to be a more purposeful way of understanding the relational byproducts of the existing 'sayings' and 'doings', as well as the voices of those involved. An incredible amount of power can be generated when there is coherence amongst the practices and the established paradigm. I want to lead a pedagogical change that better recognise the relational practices that occur in the school and intentionally orchestrates more opportunities for them. Recognising pedagogy as present across all dimensions leads to a more coherent understanding of the ecologies of a school site. Acknowledging and deliberately facilitating opportunities for staff to connect in the social space contributes positively to the wellbeing of all participants, particularly teachers. Agency and voice are cornerstones to any sustainable relationship and play a crucial role in building a democratically responsive paradigm like lifelong learning.

Thinking about instruction and what educators produce together encompasses much of the important work of schooling. Leading pedagogy together invites people to move beyond producing together. When people start reflecting upon, identifying, and evaluating the relational dynamics in their work in classrooms and staff rooms, it starts to become *us* work. *Us* work is pedagogy.

Leading collectively is about having a shared, collective purpose and connecting purpose to collective action through collective involvement or through collective leading for collective change. Leading together is integral to collective wellbeing because it is about *us*. A collective doesn't lose *me*, or just involve me, but encompasses my contribution to become our collective contribution, through carefully planned purpose translated into action. Deciding to do things together is the ultimate purpose of schooling.

Leading pedagogy together goes beyond role titles and descriptions to the heart of the practices of leading as a collective, on a particular priority at a particular moment in time. Leading pedagogy defines the real work of schooling: leading the child and leading children together in community.

Communities are About Relationships

We are currently in an era of school refusal and increased measurement and performativity through global standardised testing and poor mental health indicators for students in Australian schools. Gaps between leading and learning practices are not great for wellbeing. **We see pedagogy as leading the**

child, based on a reciprocal relationship. The purpose of this book is to ensure that reciprocal relationship is integral to teaching and learning, where children are central to the daily practices of educators, and the professional learning and communications of teachers and leaders. This might sound simple and obvious, but sometimes the simplest things are the most taken for granted. Strong communities are built by listening, understanding, and utilising everyone's voices in strategic planning, in classroom learning and professional learning. In building strong communities, leaders care deeply about the professional learning and welfare of teachers in their teams.

Professional learning can be seen as an afterthought or an add-on for teachers, and yet the style of professional learning undertaken in a school often mirrors the pedagogy taking place in classrooms. The opportunity to learn about learning and to lead learning with teachers impacts teachers and students equally. Authentic wellbeing at work comes from job satisfaction, and yet we know that many teachers are leaving the profession and middle leaders are highly stressed and burnt out. This book takes leaders through a process of collectively designing and crafting pedagogical work that is satisfying and sustainable, aligned with goals and a clear priority, by building practices that support communication, reflection, resolution, and action. These are the practices of leading learning together.

There is a lot of rhetoric around values in educational leadership policy but little examination of these values in practice. Engagement with values is an essential starting point for reforming pedagogy and wellbeing in schools, in the context of your school.

Arrangements

Over the last few years, Australian school leaders have told us about burnout and increasing workload demands for their teaching teams and themselves.

> The heavy workload and busyness of school life (especially admin) can constrain the ability to be creative and engage in bigger-picture thinking and planning.

They have told us about their struggles to implement constant change, often imposed on them with minimal consultation, and about their limited agency in managing workloads. These perceptions are echoed in international research on teacher wellbeing, such as the OECD (Organisation for Economic Co-operation and Development) Teaching and Learning International Survey. There is a sense of more and more work being added and nothing being taken away.

> People tend to be implementing things rather than understanding why they are implementing them.
> There is no articulated vision for the school or my role. There is no shared vision – siloing is strong.

School leaders have shared with us with busy timetables and school calendars that they have limited time to plan and reflect together on their values and purpose as a school. They explain how they are doing their best within their own departments but wanting more opportunities to collaborate across departments and with leaders at all levels in their schools and even to discuss daily work and students. In our work in schools, we have found that leadership can be more and less distributed in schools and that leaders clearly relished the opportunities created by professional learning to work together in thinking about their school and especially about their students. Middle leaders were ready and willing to contribute to school-level change when they felt safe to do so.

> Decisions are made ad hoc, without consultation, and then fully communicated, and without an opportunity to question them. Decisions tend to be imposed from above and ideas or concerns don't really have a place in the discussion unless it is what senior leaders want to do or discuss.
>
> We would be able to make much better decisions, changes, and create better opportunities for the students, for the staff, if they were to consult more. Rather than making decisions hastily for the sake of saving time, to reach out and tread very carefully about who, or what is at stake.

In the schools where we have worked, we have noticed that engagement has been highest when there is genuine consultation between leaders. Imposed decisions can lead to a sense of powerlessness and even resentment, leading to burnout and disengagement. Research on motivation and engagement at work provides solid evidence that this is what happens in workplaces where autonomy and psychological safety are low (Hallam et al., 2023; de Lisser et al., 2024).

When leaders are invited to have a shared purpose, they start thinking differently about how they lead together and how they work with others:

> I have stepped into a new role, and this has made me think more about leadership and working with others. We have a leadership structure that has been in place for many years. Breaking that mold or idea is hard to do. This year our school had an executive conference where the 'second in charge' of the faculty were invited. This helped strengthen another level of our school leadership while also building capacity of others. We do have forward thinking people in middle leadership roles that are committed to changing the structure of our School.

To lead pedagogy and wellbeing together, leaders need practical strategies for including shared vision, communicating, job design, and a singular priority. These ways of working together have the capacity to respect the whole child and the whole educator.

Who are We?

Each chapter of this book explores real school leadership scenarios that come from extensive work the authors have done with school leaders over several years. We have done intensive year-long work with school leadership teams in their schools, in the form of Research–Practice Partnerships, at their request. These have involved working closely with leaders, drawing upon research and evaluating the success of the professional learning intervention. We have also worked with school leadership teams and with individual leaders across Australia on research-informed professional learning on pedagogy and wellbeing for middle leaders. We teach postgraduate education students at The University of Sydney, who have shared their own middle leadership experiences. Two of our students are cited in this book, with their consent, and we would like to thank them for their insightful contributions.

The authors themselves have worked in a range of capacities, and our own research and professional experiences have influenced our writing. Christine has co-led three large Australian research projects for school middle leaders. The patterns and issues that emerged in these projects have influenced our thinking. Christine is an experienced educator and educational leader, working in schools in a range of teaching and leadership capacities over several decades. Christine worked in universities and schools, after being a Head of School, whilst completing her doctoral studies, returning to a middle leader position in a secondary school. Moving backwards and sideways gives you very different insights into leading together. Throughout her career Christine prioritised working in special education alongside her school leadership positions, often working one on one with students. Valuing the most vulnerable students in a school gives you important insights into how well a school is living its pedagogical values.

Fiona started her career as an Organisational Psychologist and later trained as a Clinical Psychologist. She has years of experience interviewing hundreds of people at all levels in multiple organisations to understand their experiences at work. She has also worked therapeutically with many people experiencing workplace stress and burnout and has run workshops on workplace wellbeing for many years. Her PhD was part of a large longitudinal study examining student wellbeing in schools. Similarly to Christine, she has worked as a team member and middle leader and in executive positions – but not in a specific order. Her experiences as a leader have informed her practices as a team member and vice versa.

This is an interdisciplinary book which brings together ideas from philosophy, sociology, and psychology. We believe that these diverse perspectives provide a more comprehensive and holistic picture of the complex problems and possibilities of leading learning and wellbeing in schools. By bringing together knowledge and practices from these different fields, we are attempting to bring a hopeful perspective to school improvement which incorporates pedagogical purpose, a systems perspective, and care for the whole person (whether they are an educator or a student).

Our shared values include

- Concern for the whole child and the whole educator
- The long-term development of people (whether they are educators or students) is more important than any individual project, just as pedagogy is more than teaching techniques.
- Leading is a collective endeavour. People have different responsibilities but are equally responsible for enacting the shared values where people are equally valued.

Finally, we believe that **everyone can make a start with themselves and their teams with what is in their control**. Often people say that they can't start, or it is not up to them, or they are waiting for someone to make the change. Being the change, in your area and acknowledging what is outside your control and what you seek to influence, is an approach that works.

Knowing, articulating, and living agreed values are essential for leading learning and wellbeing, for the formation of students and educators rather than the reforming of schools. Rather than fixing, we focus on connecting for improving by continually returning to values and purpose in leading learning together.

We connected our interdisciplinary ideas through a pedagogy and wellbeing spiral, connected with our values and our empirical work in leading pedagogy and wellbeing together (Figure 0.1). The spiral is based on the following principles about leading pedagogy and wellbeing. Trust is the foundation of leading pedagogy and wellbeing in schools. The application of trust is that participants experience psychological safety in their school. From this basis, collaboration which leads to critical reflection on practices can occur. These skills may develop capabilities in leaders, which are seen in practice as habits that people and teams develop over time. Agency and autonomy lead to engagement in work and job satisfaction. As people develop agency, they seek to solve problems and adapt their skills to new situations through job crafting that is both individual and collective. These practices come from everyone understanding their individual purpose and the collective purpose of the school, which leads to solidarity. Solidarity comes from understanding and living shared values through leading together.

None of these practices is static, which is why a spiral was chosen. As schools are places of constant change, groups of people can develop and redevelop practices in new situations. As new situations are presented, teams may go up and down the spiral. Leading is about building trust and psychological safety so that people can move together in their work. The six principles of the spiral and their correspondent applications will be explored in each of the chapters.

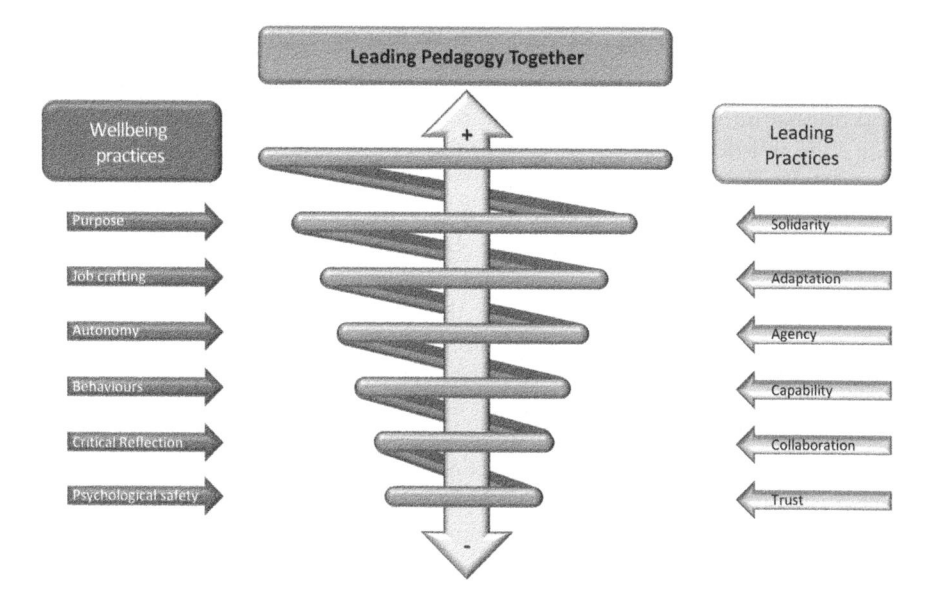

Figure 0.1 Pedagogy and wellbeing spiral.

Our work is about empathy, voice, and listening whether as researchers or as practitioners coming together from distinct disciplines. We have needed to listen to each other in writing this book and to learn about our disciplines to build a collective understanding of leading learning and wellbeing together in an interdisciplinary way. Education itself is interdisciplinary, involving sociology, psychology, pedagogy, and arts and sciences. Teaching is a series of interdisciplinary practices.

Behaviour and practice theories intertwine in interesting ways. In psychology, behaviour is defined as "an organism's activities in response to external or internal stimuli, including objectively observable activities, introspectively observable activities (see covert behavior), and nonconscious processes" (APA Dictionary of Psychology, https://dictionary.apa.org/behavior). This means that behaviour involves actions that may or may not be visible and may occur in response to either an internal (thought, emotion, belief, bodily sensation, etc.) or external (context, other people's behaviour, societal rules, etc.) event or situation.

Practice theory draws upon sociology and philosophy. As authors, we find ourselves explaining terms from psychology and sociology to each other and their similarities and differences. We believe that teachers navigate interdisciplinary concepts in their work all the time. Behaviour and practice have the capacity to complement each other if we connect theories with practices. This book seeks to bridge ideas and bring into conversation theories that interrelate that are helpful to teachers in practice.

Practice Menu: Leading Learning and Wellbeing Together

This book is about practices. Practices are simply the things that people say and do that inform how people relate to each other. Practices and people do not stand in isolation in the social space of schools. Practices are informed by cultural-discursive arrangements which include modes of communication, material economic arrangements which include elements of resourcing, and social political arrangements which are about priorities and influence. Practices and practice arrangements are informed by policy, people, and place. Practices become patterns of doing. Over time, they become habits and histories that inform practice traditions in a site (Kemmis & Smith, 2008). Practices matter because if we notice practices we can see what we are able to change.

Styles, personalities, or even culture can be limiting notions of people and leadership. When we think about someone's personality or style, we assume it is fixed and cannot be changed. Practices can change. We can say different things, do different things, and relate in new ways. We can prioritise new voices and alter cultural-discursive arrangements. We can adjust resources such as calendars, timetables, meeting times, or even buildings to enable meeting times and places or to constrain them. We can think carefully about whether the way we work is about power or solidarity in the cultural-discursive arrangements. Are everyday interactions about telling people what to do or about consensus? Understanding practices is a way of reflecting on people and sites. Understanding practices can highlight where purpose may look different from action. Practices are ultimately about hope: the hope for change.

Practice theory is closely related with Action Research (Lewin, 1947), which is a process of solving problems of practice. Action research cycles have been used in schools for many decades to support teachers to use research-informed practices. In an Action Research Cycle, participants actively engage in research and problem-solving with others, in a cycle of planning, actioning, observing, and reflecting. These look like our research practice partnerships and like our cycle of collective job crafting found in Chapter 8.

Each chapter in the book has a practice menu related to the specific themes and practices they address, informed by our research. The practice menu is loosely derived from *the table of invention of practices* (Kemmis et al., 2014), which is a tool that practice theory researchers use to analyse the practices in a site. The practice menus are designed to highlight key practices that each chapter covered for leading pedagogy and wellbeing together, alongside key questions.

We have chosen to call them menus so that you can select the practices most relevant to your site rather than have us prescribe ways of leading learning and wellbeing for you. The final chapter also explains how practices also exist together in ecologies of practices that together inform each other.

We understand our purpose when we return to our values. Critical educational praxis is action informed by values. Living our values involves critical reflection, learning, listening, (Mahon et al., 2019, p. 2), and leading together so that shared values shape shared vision. Opportunities for educators to meet are essential for developing these practices.

Professional learning that makes a difference to all educators supports the development of critical praxis in active participants. This is made possible through learning and leadership arrangements that support power, agency, and trust (Francisco et al., 2021). Therefore, fresh understandings about leading, wellbeing, and pedagogy are integral to leading learning together.

Summary of Key Points

- Our book is about the whole child and the whole educator.
- We see pedagogy and wellbeing as parts of a whole rather than as separate domains.
- We emphasise the importance of collective approaches and of viewing leading as a set of practices aligned with values.

Questions

Let's get started with what matters. What questions do you have? Here are some to start with:

- What is it like to work in my school?
- What does my school value and how do I know?
- How do I connect with others in my school in my role? What else could we do?
- What external and internal conditions influence leading together in my school?
- Who owns the school vision? Where is my part in it?
- How do my actions and those of others relate to our vision and purpose?
- What brings solidarity in our school?

Conclusion

When our values and habits align, we can think about how to take the first steps to change in an ongoing process of continuous questioning, reflecting, and returning to values and purpose. This cycle defines the direction of this book.

The introductory chapter helped educators to reflect on their purpose by understanding *what's our why?* It briefly outlined the current leadership and wellbeing context in schools in Australia. We outlined the education values we see as essential to engaging in the ideas in the book for pedagogical reform. We see reforming as less about individual leaders in schools fixing and more about connecting for improving by continually returning to values and purpose. We introduced the Pedagogy and Wellbeing Spiral to support practice.

The emphasis of this book is on doing: on building habits and practices from clear principles of leading pedagogy and wellbeing together. These principles are derived from our backgrounds in educational leadership and organisational psychology. This book is a deeply practical book with strategies for communicating, job design, and leading pedagogy through wellbeing.

To grow and sustain leading together, our book involves five simple questions on a continuous cycle. Chapters 1 and 2 outline Step 1: 'Who are we?' and involve clearly understanding your school environment, your teachers, your students, and your community. Step 2: 'How do we work together?' is outlined in Chapters 3 and 4 and involves a mutual understanding of each other and how everyone works together. Step 3: 'What do we need?' is outlined in Chapters 5, 6, and 7 and supports how schools can identify problems and practices that need to change. Step 4: 'How can we get there?' is outlined in Chapter 8 and looks at the process of change in schools. Step 5: 'How are we going?' is also examined in Chapter 8 and evaluates the outcome, the process, and the shared purposes of leading pedagogy. Step 5 leads back to Step 1 in a continuing process. This process emphasises intentional reflection, sustainability, and continuous improvement. There is no end point.

Synopsis

The introductory chapter has introduced the purpose of the book and its key interdisciplinary ideas, including pedagogy, wellbeing, leading, and practice. It advocates for why leading together in practice is so important for pedagogy and for the wellbeing of students, teachers, and leaders in the context of schools today.

Chapter 1 is about collective involvement. It debunks the popular idea that leaders are heroes and singular beings on a mission to rescue education and explains why these assumptions conflict with the collective education project. It introduces leading principles that enable collective practices to be applied through a school leadership practices diagnosis.

Chapter 2 is about collective pedagogy. Authenticity and self-awareness supports educators to consider their strengths, gifts, and contexts and how these can be utilised in leading learning and how they form the basis of wellbeing practices in connection with others.

Chapter 3 is about collective wellbeing. The chapter looks closely at the habits that enable wellbeing, and Chapter 3 looks at trust as a fundamental habit to be practised for psychological safety to remain embedded in the work of teams. Capabilities are also explored.

Chapter 4 focuses on collective leading. The chapter is about respecting others and taking responsibility for leading learning, returning to original meanings of pedagogy: to lead the child and implications for learning and wellbeing through trust and psychological safety.

Chapter 5 is about collective responsibility. This chapter makes practical suggestions for leading change together in a school through key skills and practices that enable effective communication and how these skills develop individual autonomy and collective agency. The type of communicating we do represents the leading that we value. Work recovery is also addressed.

Chapter 6 is about collective change. The chapter examines our motivations for doing leadership roles and how to understand and support agency, engagement, and motivation. Collective job crafting is explored as a way of maximising gifts and strengths adapting to the needs of specific school contexts.

Chapter 7 is about collective purpose. It focuses on solidarity of purpose through agency, engagement and motivation. Culturally responsive leadership practices are prioritised through Aboriginal perspectives.

Chapter 8 is about collective job crafting. The chapter addresses the sustainability of practices and the long game of leading pedagogy and wellbeing in schools. It concludes with leaders being intentional in leading learning together and the inspiration of influence, the value of feedback, and the importance of understanding control. We suggest possibilities for starting this work, beginning from the beginning rather than an end point and realising that the work of leading learning together well never ends.

Overall, our book is designed for school leadership teams interested in working cohesively together in the continuous project of knowing students and how they learn. Our work draws upon educational leadership theories and psychological theories infrequently connected in educational leadership in Australia. It is designed to support leaders to create sustainable, productive learning environments where wellbeing and learning are integral for teachers and students. This book is about how to get started with what matters.

References

de Lisser, R., Dietrich, M.S., Spetz, J., Ramanujam, R., Lauderdale, J, Stolldorf, D.P. (2024). Psychological safety is associated with better work environment and lower levels of clinician burnout, *Health Affairs Scholar*, 2(7), qxae091, DOI:10.1093/haschl/qxae091

Francisco, S., Forssten Seiser, A., & Grice, C. (2021). Professional learning that enables the development of critical praxis. *Professional Development in Education*, 49(5), 938–952. DOI:10.1080/19415257.2021.1879228

Hallam, K.T., Popovic N., & Karimi, L. (2023). Identifying the key elements of psychologically safe workplaces in healthcare settings. *Brain Sciences*, 13(10), 1450. DOI:10.3390/brainsci13101450. PMID: 37891818; PMCID: PMC10605501.

Kemmis, S., & Smith, T. (2008). Praxis and praxis development. In S. Kemmis & T. Smith (eds.) *Enabling Praxis: Challenges for Education.* (pp. 3–13). Rotterdam: Sense.

Kemmis, S., Wilkinson, J., Edwards-Groves, C., Hardy, I., Grootenboer, P., & Bristol, L. (2014). *Changing Practices, Changing Education.* Singapore: Springer.

Lewin, K. (1947). *Field Theory in Social Science.* New York: Harper & Row.

Mahon, K., Heikkinen, H.L.T., & Huttunen, R., 2019. Critical educational praxis in university ecosystems: Enablers and constraints. *Pedagogy, Culture & Society, 27*(3), 463–480. DOI:10.1080/14681366.2018.1522663

1 Understanding the Context of Your School

What is it like to lead in your school? Where the introductory chapter looked at the broader context of education, this chapter focuses in on your school context and its departments, stages, classes, and individual students. Your school's unique context informs the collective purpose of your school, underpinned by its values. Schools with an imposed vision and divergent purposes may have leaders who operate in silos. If practices are established to enable leaders to communicate and work together, schools with a shared vision and a collective purpose may have leaders who are more able to lead together in practice, inviting collective responsibility. Chapter 1 focuses on understanding your school leadership context. In this chapter, understanding the leadership context of your school is less about where your school is, or who attends, and more about what leadership looks like. This chapter invites leaders to ask several diagnostic questions about leading in your school, individually and collectively. These include *What is my leadership role like? What does leadership look like in our school?* and *Where are we at with working together?* These questions explore people's perceptions about their roles and how people work together in practice, within and beyond hierarchy.

Examples from Schools

Pelé famously remarked, "No individual can win a game by himself." The introductory chapter highlighted the increasing workload issues in schools today. These need to change and so does the way that workload is perpetuated in schools by educators working in silos or alone. Leading together is the leading that schools are meant for. This chapter shifts our focus from individual roles to the practices of leading learning and wellbeing together and our collective responsibility. The practices in this chapter invite leaders to identify places where they are working individually and to think creatively about where they could work collectively.

Juncture School is a nurturing school where supporting student wellbeing is core to its values. Their new principal is establishing a strategic vision for the school that prioritises student wellbeing and academic attainment by knowing and valuing every student. School leaders are involved in the strategic

DOI: 10.4324/9781003564843-2

planning, but the principal sets the strategy. The senior leaders could have decided to implement projects by themselves, but they recognise the importance of the middle leadership team being involved in enacting the vision in practice.

Middle leaders at Juncture School are responsible for contributing to the strategic vision by "ensuring that they're drawn into creating a shared vision and understanding the direction together", according to one senior leader. When they are invited in to conceptualise the vision alongside other leaders, everyone is aware of what is within their control. As one senior leader explains, "It's not being done to them, we're walking alongside and supporting the middle leaders with a shared vision and direction." Middle leaders require skills that enable them to enact the vision in practice with their teams. As another senior leader shares, "They need to know how to implement continuous improvement and what that looks like. They need to know how to observe lessons, how to approach their teams and how to bring about a shared vision."

Middle leaders at Juncture School are being invited into the school vision for the first time. This signified a shift in their leadership responsibilities as the leadership team were evolving new practices for leading together. Senior leaders were recognising how to support middle leaders to interpret the school vision and connect it with projects they created with their teams. As one senior leader understands, "Middle leaders work close to the ground with a big teaching load, on small projects that contribute to the wider strategic vision." Once these initiatives develop, the sphere of influence of middle leaders could grow at Juncture School as they realise their collective purpose. They are in a developing phase for leading together.

Tumult School

Tumult School is a caring school community, and students come from a diverse range of backgrounds and cultures. Teachers are committed and comfortable, and people stay for a long time. People are accustomed to doing things in a hierarchical way for a traditional command and control principal. When a new principal arrives, middle leaders are uncertain of the expectations of their role and unsure how to lead pedagogy through learning and wellbeing together.

> It's a significant shift, a different way of doing things. I'd call it a cultural shift. There was no trust before. It was a culture of 'tell me what to do and I'll do it', but then, also, middle leaders not feeling they had a voice. As a consequence, there is no coherent understanding of the role of middle leaders in our school. Senior leaders view middle leaders narrowly and this guides the low expectations that they have of them. Middle leaders only know how to be exemplary administrators. They're highly organized and efficient, but there is also a sense of helplessness from some of them. I still don't think we've nailed that sense of their own leadership identity…

Middle leaders at Tumult School have not been seen as leaders, so they do not have an individual or a collective leadership identity. There is work to be done on understanding self, and others, to gain a shared understanding of learning and wellbeing before they can lead together. For this reason, Tumult School is in a pre-readiness phase of leading together.

Primed School

Primed School is a contemporary, high-achieving school with dedicated teachers and middle leaders who are creative and who conform to the expectations set for them by Senior leaders for their students. There is a high level of control.

> Heads of department work with their teams implementing initiatives that come from the senior leadership team. They make sure that everything is being done as it should be. Most senior leaders have good relationships with middle leaders. However, in more recent times, there has been little discussion or consultation, leaving out people who could make valuable contributions, excellent decisions and make changes really work well. Middle leaders need good skills supporting students in challenging situations particularly with our parents here. That's why middle leaders tend to call themselves the meat in the sandwich. Having to mediate between the expectations of parents, and what the children need, want, and are capable of. This is why we worked with you, to build middle leaders feelings of being valued and recognising their competencies. We have great relationships between our middle leaders; however, they don't really know where they are in the leadership structure. Our middle leaders are very strong, but they are underutilised, because they are at times ignored and forgotten, in the communication, collaboration and consultation. People tend to be implementing things without understanding why. I think middle leaders would say that their ability to effect change is just within their team. There is no opportunity beyond their team. They also feel overworked and bogged down. I think the middle leader role is a powerful, interesting one. It's a central role, a difficult role sometimes. Sometimes, as the name suggests, they are caught in the middle.

Middle leaders at Primed School are frequently navigating and mediating the expectations of senior leaders, students, and parents. This school is doing many things well, but their middle leaders are caught in the middle. They can grow leadership within their own department silos, where middle leaders can build teams where *we* lead. Primed School is in a readiness phase to lead together, but to lead collectively, the identity of middle leaders needs to be valued. Increased consultation and collaboration would build agency, trust, and an *us* identity.

Eager School

Eager School is a tight school community in a low socioeconomic area where dedicated educators work together. A middle leader found us and took the initiative to organise a Research-Practice Partnership (R-PP) for their school.

> Middle leaders have one of the most important, if not the most important roles in school. They are at the forefront of what happens with students in the classrooms as well as supporting staff. They are in charge of ensuring that all our initiatives and our strategic plan goes ahead. They have a direct impact on pretty much every facet of the school. We have an approachable senior leadership team and if people have an issue, or if they want to change something or improve things, they are confident that they can come and have a chat. We're open to changing things. So, they have strong agency to create change. We're so invested in the school. We call ourselves a family and love the school and students. The connection between each other is important. Having that trust between leaders. I love this school; I love this place. I'm so excited to see what happens with the team next. At the end of this year, we build our new plan, and I know that everything that you have taught us, and we worked on, we'll be putting into action. We're also in a time where there's talk about increasing our workload and that has caused a lot of concern. Middle leaders have voiced their concerns. They are going to struggle even more with workload in these conditions. I see it as my role to create the environment where middle leaders can do the work that they need to do and do it in a way that is supportive and that they can collaborate and learn.

Eager School is a place where the contribution of everyone is valued and this is demonstrated by the principals' close interactions with the whole leadership team and the senior leader's respect for the work of middle leaders. As a result, middle leaders were committed to whole-school initiatives despite tight workloads because strong trusting relationships built a whole-school commitment to leading together for a school community people loved. The leaders worked together to develop a shared vision leading together, outlining four key areas that they wanted to work on, including reducing the workload of their middle leaders. Eager School were in an improving phase.

Connecting Research and Practice

In each of the examples from the schools above, a readiness phase has been mentioned. Day and Grice (2019) developed *The Middle Leadership Framework* from participant data in an Australian research project to capture how ready a school is to develop their middle leaders. Leadership teams can use the table to diagnose their readiness to lead together and develop their middle leaders. Leaders determine where their school is placed in the framework (Figure 1.1).

20 *Leading Learning and Wellbeing Together*

A Framework for Diagnosing School Readiness for Middle Leadership Development

	Pre-Readiness Phase Practices that constrain middle leading	**Developing Phase** Practices that enable and constrain the development of middle leading	**Improving Phase** Practices that develop and enable sustainable middle leading
Cultural Norms	Middle leaders' expectations and aspirations are restricted to their own area of influence	Middle leading is distributed in existing spheres of influence	Middle leaders lead collaboratively *beyond* the middle together with others
	Irregular meetings within middle leadership team	Regular meetings within middle leadership teams, but little focus upon pedagogy	Middle leaders meet their team regularly to discuss relationships between teaching and learning and individual student progress and achievement
	Miscommunication from minimal shared language	Shared language within select teams translating vision into understanding and action	Shared language across the school resulting in clear understandings, support, and action
	No scheme for mutual classroom teaching and learning observation	Some areas have schemes for mutual classroom teaching and learning observation	All areas have schemes for mutual classroom teaching and learning observation
	No middle leader mentoring or preparation for mentoring	Some middle leader mentoring or preparation for mentoring	Middle leader mentoring across the school
Improvement Practices	No participation in curriculum and practice inquiry projects	Occasional participation in inquiry projects which target middle leaders' own and whole school needs	Regular participation in projects with other middle leaders which target whole school development needs
	No collegial consideration of planning, teaching and learning and assessment	Occasional collegial consideration of planning, teaching and learning and assessment	Regular collegial consideration of school-wide planning, teaching and learning and assessment
	Minimal understanding and utilisation of student progress data in planning classroom teaching	Data utilisation led by the executive and facilitated by middle leaders	Data utilisation led by middle leaders with the executive and teachers in the middle leading team
	Student progress and outcomes not formally discussed	Student progress regularly discussed, but uncertain impact upon student outcomes	Student progress and outcomes regularly discussed in association with of teaching planning and practices
Building Social Capital	Principals and executive do not provide time for middle leaders to meet together to discuss issues of teaching and learning	Principals and executive provide time upon request for middle leaders to meet	Principals and executive provide time for middle leaders to lead teams in *and* beyond the middle
	Little evidence of relational trust in middle leadership teams	Mixed evidence of relational trust in middle leadership teams	Evidence of widespread relational and collective trust across the school
	Leadership is delegated* within teams	Evidence of communities of practice within the distribution of leadership in some teams	Strong evidence of school-wide communities of practice and extensive leadership distribution
	No participation in school wide decision-making about curriculum and pedagogy	Occasional participation in school wide decision-making about curriculum and pedagogy	Regular participation in school wide decision-making about curriculum and pedagogy
	Irregular provision of opportunities for sustained professional development using external facilitation	Limited provision of jointly planned opportunities for sustained professional development, using external facilitation	Regular jointly planned opportunities for sustained professional development using external facilitation

*'Delegation' implies restricted powers of decision-making and autonomy, in contrast to distribution which implies extended powers of decision making and autonomy

Figure 1.1 Middle Leadership Framework (Day & Grice, 2019). The Middle Leadership Framework is shared with permission of the Association of Independent Schools New South Wales (AISNSW).

The framework maps school leaders' readiness to lead together through three distinct areas, or practice arrangements. It provides them clear ideas for improvement practices and enables leaders to see how the sum of these practices demonstrated the extent to which they are leading collectively at a given point in time in their school.

The Theory of Practice Architectures

Leading pedagogy and wellbeing in schools involves people leading together reciprocally, be they teachers, leaders, or indeed students. It is inadequate to think about leading in schools through the lens of leadership roles alone or by thinking about individuals as leaders. The theory of practice architectures (Kemmis et al., 2014; Wilkinson, 2021) conceptualises leading as a practice that happens in the spaces between people, opening new possibilities for understanding the everyday practices of leading in schools. **We see leading as a set of practices that can be enacted by anyone, regardless of formal position, and that happen in the spaces between people and you can see it in action**.

One way of imagining leading as a practice is to conceptualise leading as a decentred practice. The leaders at Eager School chose key areas to work on together based on purpose, making the work less about who and more about why and how. In this way, they decentred traditional understandings of leading (Grice et al., 2023) like a hero or martyr and instead focused on practices that enabled them to plan and lead collectively.

For a long time, educators have celebrated the heroic leader. School leaders make a difference to the wellbeing of their students every day. We should celebrate the work of heroes. However, so much of what is achieved in schools happens through people working together. Leading pedagogy through learning and wellbeing is difficult or even impossible to achieve without a collective. Schools highly value teamwork in students and yet school leadership teams risk falling short of the value of teamwork. In working collectively, we look after the burnt out martyr leader, working alone. Images of heroes and martyrs come from our *anglophone*, Western views of schooling that emphasise leadership as a role with a hierarchy of command (Wilkinson et al., 2021; Kemmis, 2022). Role descriptions can provide necessary clarity, but individual role descriptions do not always support people to work in increasingly volatile circumstances in schools as leaders navigate the rapidly changing landscape in education today, nor how to understand students and how they learn together, nor the collective endeavour of workplace wellbeing. We employ practice theory to frame this book to help leaders connect what they do, or don't do, with what they could do. In this way, the theory of practice architectures (Kemmis et al., 2014) is a theory of change that focuses on the practices of leading, rather than the leader, so that the interactions between people can be analysed and understood in practice. Understanding practices enables us to see in fine grain what can be changed between us. It is a reflective, critical, and hopeful approach.

All schools have values statements and mission statements, expected to be lived by their students and rarely questioned in the practices of their leaders.

Asking *Who are we?* returns us to our values, and what we value can be found in the artefacts of a school. The school strategy outlines the vision and mission of a school. Role descriptions outline the value of work that leaders do. Policies, the size of a school, the upkeep of buildings and resources, and the communities that schools serve show what we value. School priorities demonstrate their commitment to pedagogy through learning and wellbeing. This book is about questioning who we are and why we do things here, to realign our values and purpose with practice, which is praxis: moral purpose in action.

Leading, Not Leadership

School leaders we have worked with have told us that there is work to do in understanding leadership in their schools. Most middle leaders and many senior leaders believe it is time to *distribute* leadership (Spillane, 2006) in their schools, to invite people to work together. We have noticed that schools seem to be stuck in historical leadership patterns which may take the form of a "benevolent dictatorship" or a not so benevolent one. Other schools are caught in how distributing can be practically achieved within heavy workloads and strong hierarchies, even if sharing or distributing leadership is desired. We have noticed a cavernous distance between senior leaders and middle leaders in some schools where '*us and them*' language pervades. Senior leaders talk of middle leaders *just needing to do* an initiative, and middle leaders speak of lack of consultation on decisions.

Leaders are tasked with reforming schools, and yet given the workforce issues in schools, this can be very challenging. It is a popular notion that you need to find the people who will take on the initiative to create much-needed change in the school. These people are known as *change champions*, where others are seen as *dead wood*. Jim Collins (2001) wrote a seminal business management book, *Good to Great*, where he introduces the concept of a *flywheel*, understanding that the process of change is about relentless hard work. Change is a process, and we also use a flywheel for working collectively in Chapter 8. Collins (2001) invites leaders to "get the right people on the bus, the wrong people off the bus, and the right people in the right seats" (p. 41). This is where our values diverge. We understand that people have talents that need to be nurtured and that school leaders should identify the gifts of educators and give them opportunities to lead. However, this corporate workforce metaphor has been used pervasively by school leaders to raise standards and is problematised by Courtney and Gunter (2015) for treating teachers as disposable. In schools, everyone belongs on the bus, and that is the whole point of schooling. We assume that teaching is a profession and that educators need to be respected, valued, mentored, and involved in decision-making because pedagogical work is shared. That also means that teachers need to act professionally and that students need to take responsibility. However, students, teachers, and leaders also need nurturing. Quality teaching and learning can be sustained through long-term initiatives that invite everyone to participate and that support their growth, development, and learning, and this is the core purpose of schooling.

School leadership policy and discussion today celebrate the heroic and hard-working leader, at any level, who sets a vision for reform through rigour, improvement, and change. The hero of reform is the individual. This form of individual leadership is perpetuated in schools through position descriptions and promotions. This leads to individuals believing that it was *me* who led the initiative. Leadership roles tell us who leads but not when, where, or why leading happens or how leading is shared beyond people with roles. A positional stance tells us about people's positions but may not support leaders to work across teams where middle leaders or teacher leaders might need to step beyond their department or classroom to influence school-wide change. What if we thought about how *we* did it, by exploring what happens in practice, not just what we say we do in roles. Leadership myths fall apart in practice when they fail to capture the real practices of leading that are tested during reform. School leaders are dedicated, committed individuals. If leaders saw themselves as collective rather than single heroic leaders, would their individual wellbeing, as well as the collective wellbeing of others, improve?

We all know that there are times when role-based leaders need to direct. Directing is important, particularly in matters of safety. There are times when leaders need to be direct, instructional, and clear, particularly when it comes to matters of safety, legislation, deadlines, and orderliness. Compliance should be contained as a relatively small part of leading a school, so that there is room for the true purpose of being at school: leading learning together.

Role-based leadership tends to lead towards directing over distributing. It can be easier to use coercion and control because you can. Directing is efficient and can even be welcomed by busy teachers whilst also rejected by others who seek to lead pedagogy and wellbeing with you. If you are a middle leader trying to build initiatives, *command and control* is a risk. As teachers say of middle leaders, "you are one of us". If we want to reduce disengagement, disenchantment, and burnout and increase motivation, reimagining the practices of leading together in reciprocal practice may help us all to build pedagogical change in schools.

Research–Practice Partnerships

Research-Practice Partnerships (Coburn et al., 2021; Coburn and Penuel, 2016) involve researchers and school leaders working together, over a sustained and agreed period of time, to reach a shared objective. Our goal was to support middle leaders to lead pedagogy and wellbeing together. R-PPs involve extensive consultation, bespoke aspects of professional learning, and shared evaluation. They are *done with* rather than *done to* initiatives that are established to enable leaders within a school to lead together themselves without the need for ongoing consultation. Some schools are more ready than others to work together as a whole leadership team. Some schools have limited agency for middle leaders or low psychological safety where others are growing autonomy and collectivity.

In each of our R-PPs, schools have reached out to us for support. We have also worked closely with middle leaders across Australia through professional learning workshops and with leaders enrolled in our Master of Educational Leadership program. Throughout the book, we draw upon the experiences of school leaders who have shared their insights with us.

The overarching goal of our partnerships was for leaders to work well together to support the development of people, pedagogy, and wellbeing in their school. These goals were specifically aligned with the strategic plans of each school. Our bespoke work developed coherence over time in each context. The aim was for leaders to develop a collective framework for long-term change, as they made decisions about their interactions, cultural norms, and improvement practices and develop knowledge and skills that could enable them to lead learning together in a sustainable way.

Our R-PPs sought to build practical change by enabling school leaders and their teams to collectively design and craft satisfying and sustainable work aligned with goals, building habits that support communication, reflection, resolution, and action. We supported leaders to reflect on their shared purpose and to move beyond themselves to the purpose of knowing students and how they learn. The process involved moving schools away from fixed and linear forms of change towards relational change. As school leaders developed a collective framework for long-term change, they decided upon individual and collective habits depending upon the school's readiness for change. Leaders developed knowledge and skills during professional learning sessions that could enable them to lead learning together in a sustainable way.

R-PPs are centred on a continuous research and evaluation framework (Henrick et al., 2017) where the quality can be challenging to assess (Welsh, 2021). We built trust with middle leaders in our R-PPs. The extent to which we could build partnership trust was dependent upon the connections we had with the senior leadership team. We shared the decision-making with middle and senior leadership by creating bespoke programs each time, with some similar elements based on the specific needs of their leaders. Interviews and surveys with participants gave us valuable insights into the impact of professional learning sessions so that we could adjust the information that we covered. We listened to their shared goals and helped them to formulate meaningful objectives. The diverse expertise of school leaders came out in discussion protocols that enabled participation from all partners. These practices build trust over time. Over time, we became aware of the strengths and limitations of partnering from a researcher perspective. We knew that we could not control change within the school and understood that our role was to create spaces for learning and reflection where schools chose their future directions. We were also able to provide anonymised data to schools, based upon feedback from leaders. Our work translates research in meaningful ways through the collective job crafting process that is outlined in this book.

Research and professional learning opportunities supported leaders to grow together, but the extent to which they were able to grow together was dependent upon the leadership conditions, interactions, and beliefs within each of the schools. Working intensively with three schools taught us very powerful lessons about what enables or constrains leading together in a school and therefore what can constrain collective job crafting.

Leading in Practice

This chapter invites leaders to reflect on their individual and collective leadership purpose and practices. The following tasks support shared understandings of leadership practices in your school.

Task 1: Metaphor Task

Invite Middle and Senior leaders to consider what metaphors they might use to conceptualise middle leadership. The responses that people give in drawings, images, and words tell you about how they see and understand their role and other people's roles and the strengths and barriers in their leadership. Metaphors have included being a meat in the sandwich, heavy lifting like shopping bags, and many others.

Task 2: The Middle Leadership Framework

A middle leadership framework was developed by Day and Grice (2019) to capture the practices of middle leading and the readiness that groups of leaders had for professional learning in middle leading. The framework focuses on the practices that leaders do together rather than roles and maps school leaders' readiness to work together through three distinct areas, or practice arrangements. We used this as a self-diagnostic tool in our R-PPs for leaders themselves to determine where they thought their school was placed in their own school context. It gave them immediate ideas of practices they could work on and enabled them to see how the sum of these practices amounts to the extent to which teams are collaboratively working and learning together. Ultimately, the framework can tell leaders about their own practice context for leading pedagogy and wellbeing.

Task 3: Lolly/Sweets/Candy Task: What Does Leadership Look Like In Your School?

Roberts and Woods (2018) conducted a study where they ask leadership teams to represent what leadership looks like in their school using craft materials in dot and line shapes. We use lollies/sweets/candy in our R-PPs, such as musk sticks, snakes, smarties, and other soft jellies, and invite leaders to eat the evidence, after discussing it with us and viewing other people. School principals tend to build hierarchies, or lines of command. We have seen Deputies map holarchies, or circles of collaboration. Responses of middle leaders are mixed. They often design barrier images, with lollies that represent obstacles to team leadership, holarchies, or hierarchies, or they build creative singular images of themselves, such as a smiley face representing themselves as resilient. Leaders infrequently draw students or parents, which we find interesting in a school.

Our research findings align with those of Roberts and Woods (2018), especially the types of images seen, and build upon their work in recognising patterns of different viewpoints from different leaders over time. Regardless of what leaders build, everyone is correct. Perception is reality. What they design is exactly how they see leadership in their school and what they believe they enact. To change habits, people need to be able to see different people's perspectives and to imagine the possibilities of leading together. Collective job crafting is a process that supports leading together. The practices developed in the lolly task enable people to see what is in the imaginary, so that they can start problem-solving together.

Practice Menu

The practice menu invites leaders to reflect upon their current leading practices and provides questions they could ask of themselves or their teams to

Current practices	*Questions about practice arrangements*	*Suggested practices for application*
Sayings (communication) What do people say leading looks like in our school? Do we say what we do and do what we say?	***Cultural-discursive arrangements*** How clear are our school vision and mission to us? Who speaks and who is unheard in our school? What purpose do meetings and interactions have? Are they administrative or innovative? How do we communicate the most? What works and what needs changing so we can lead together?	1. Complete the metaphor task to consider what people say about leading, particularly middle leading. 2. Consider what leading looks like in your school by completing the lolly task based on Roberts and Woods' (2018) research on leadership as collage.
Doings Do I understand what my role is? What does leadership look like in my school? How do things change around here? How ready are we to work together? What practices could we adopt/change?	***Material-economic arrangements*** How do we meet to do our work? How does the physical layout of our school support or hinder us in leading together? How do the resources (e.g., timetable, calendar, and learning/risk management systems) enable and constrain leading together? Does what we do relate to the school strategy?	3. Think about how I organise my own role. Are there things I prioritise and things I avoid in my everyday work? 4. Use the middle leadership framework (Day and Grice, 2019) to consider how ready our school is to lead learning and wellbeing together.

(Continued)

Current practices	Questions about practice arrangements	Suggested practices for application
Relatings What metaphors describe middle leadership for us? How are we connected as leaders? Who works with whom? What is hierarchy/holarchy like at our place, and how does it work/not work for us?	*Social-political arrangements* How is the school strategy enacted and by whom? Who has the permission/power to enact change at our school? What is the collective purpose of our leadership team? How can we support leaders to develop collective purpose together?	
Dispositions (habitus) How do we see leadership here? How ready are we to lead together? Do we have any heroes/martyrs, compliance officers/coaches/captains? Do I know my/our purpose?	*Practice traditions* How do we do things around here? What is most important to us? What is static or changing? Does my purpose align with the collective purpose of our school?	

Summary of Key Points

- *Who are we?* and *Where are we?* are powerful questions that leaders ask to understand their school context and their leadership context.
- The images we have in our minds about leadership become what we enact.
- Leadership is more than an individual role title or hierarchy. Leading is a practice that happens in the spaces between people. This helps us to think about what leading together can look like.
- If we identify and focus on the practices of leading, we can invite change by working out where people are working individually and where they are working collectively and why.
- Your context can enable and constrain leading together through what you do, what you say, and how you relate and the surrounding arrangements that determine those things.
- The introductory chapter introduced the idea of values and purpose. This chapter invites you to think about the collective purpose of your school.
- What leadership really looks like in your school is the way you live collective purpose.

- Workloads are increasing in schools today. These need to change and so does the way that workload is perpetuated in schools by educators working in silos or alone. The middle leadership framework in this chapter helps leaders to identify where they are working individually and where they could work collectively and perhaps where they are even working together already.
- Understanding leading is integral to beginning to lead collectively.
- Research–Practice Partnerships support schools to develop research-informed practice through clear goals, professional learning sessions, and ongoing evaluation processes.
- The leadership practices outlined in this chapter are based on empirical research.

change practices in their school, connecting the idea of context with ideas of leading in Chapter 1.

References

Coburn, C.E., & Penuel, W.R. (2016). Research–practice partnerships in education: Outcomes, dynamics, and open questions. *Educational Researcher*, 45(1), 48–54. DOI:10.3102/0013189X16631750

Coburn, C.E., Penuel, W.R., & Farrell, C.C. (2021). Fostering educational improvement with research-practice partnerships. *Phi Delta Kappan*, 102(7), 14–19. DOI:10.1177/00317217211007332

Collins, J. (2001). *Good to Great: Why Some Companies Make the Leap and Others Don't*. New York: Random House.

Courtney, S.J., & Gunter, H.M. (2015). *Get off my bus!* School leaders, vision work and the elimination of teachers. *International Journal of Leadership in Education*, 18(4), 395–417. DOI:10.1080/13603124.2014.992476

Day, C., & Grice, C. (2019). *Investigating the Influence and Impact of Leading from the Middle: A School-based Strategy for Middle Leaders in Schools*. The University of Sydney. https://hdl.handle.net/2123/19972

Grice, C., Forssten Seiser, A., & Wilkinson, J. (2023). Decentring pedagogical leadership: Educational leading as a pedagogical practice. *Journal of Educational Administration and History*, 55(1), 89–107. DOI:10.1080/00220620.2022.2163381

Henrick, E.C., Cobb, P., Penuel, W.R., Jackson, K., & Clark, T. (2017). *Assessing Research-Practice Partnerships: Five Dimensions of Effectiveness*. New York: William T. Grant Foundation.

Kemmis, S. (2022). *Transforming Practices: Changing the World with the Theory of Practice Architectures*. Singapore: Springer.

Kemmis, S., Wilkinson, J., Edwards-Groves, C., Hardy, I., Grootenboer, P., & Bristol, L. (2014). *Changing Practices, Changing Education*. Singapore: Springer.

Roberts, A., & Woods, P.A. (2018). Theorising the value of collage in exploring educational leadership, *British Educational Research Journal*, 44(2), 626–642. DOI:10.1002/berj.3451

Spillane, J. P. (2006). *Distributed Leadership.* San Francisco, CA: Jossey-Bass Publishers.
Welsh, R.O. (2021). Assessing the quality of education research through its relevance to practice: An integrative review of research-practice partnerships. *Review of Research in Education,* 45(1), 170–194. DOI:10.3102/0091732X20985082
Wilkinson, J. (2021). *Educational Leadership through a Practice Lens: Practice Matters.* Singapore: Springer.
Wilkinson, J., Walsh, L., Keddie, A., & Longmuir, F. (2021). The emotional labour of educational leading: A practice lens. In J. Wilkinson (Ed.), *Educational Leadership through a Practice Lens: Practice Matters* 1st ed. (Educational Leadership Theory). (pp. 157–183). Singapore: Springer.

2 Knowing Yourself and Others

Who are you and *what are you good at?* These are questions we often ask students because growth and proficiency are at the heart of the purposes of schooling. How often do we take the time to reflect on ourselves as pedagogues and leaders of learning and wellbeing? Chapter 2 assists leaders in building self-awareness as the foundation for leading learning and wellbeing. Pedagogy is about knowing yourself and others. Self-awareness is integral to pedagogy because it involves knowing how we see ourselves and how others see us. It includes both intrapersonal and interpersonal awareness. School leaders are encouraged to think about how they understand people (including students) in their school. Critical self-reflection skills build knowledge of self and others to lead others well in learning and wellbeing or pedagogy. Pedagogy in Greek means to *lead the child*. Leaders are encouraged to know themselves as educators, so that they can bring their whole selves as educators to school and lead children. Leaders are encouraged to reflect on their pedagogical gifts and, by knowing their pedagogical values and purpose, connect these beliefs with their thoughts, emotions, and actions.

Examples from Schools

Self-awareness and Shared Awareness

Katherine Mansfield (Notebook 30, 1921 cited Murry, 1889–1957) wrote, "I want, by understanding myself, to understand others." Knowing yourself, and others is key to leading pedagogy and wellbeing. At Bradbury School, there was a change in principal. The previous principal had led the school for many years and was expected to make every decision. The school had grown during that time, and a new principal sought to recognise and develop the leadership capacities of middle and senior leaders throughout the school. These leaders were accustomed to managing, not leading, and given that they had no former opportunities to be self-aware leaders, they found it difficult to understand what leading might look like in practice, nor leading together. A lack of understanding of leading permeated the school leadership team. Senior leaders expected middle leaders to manage learning and wellbeing in the same ways they had always done. They, too, could not see how to lead together. It was difficult to know where to begin. It looked like this:

> There is no coherent understanding of the role of middle leaders across the executive team. The narrow way some senior leaders view middle leadership guides the expectations they have of middle leaders. If you ran a tight ship when you were a middle leader and you did assessment and curriculum a certain way, and everyone was happy, then that dictates your expectations of the middle leaders you lead. Other senior leaders recognised that they needed to support middle leaders to realise their competencies and build their feelings of being valued. The tension between the expectations that middle leaders should manage or lead resulted in a level of exhaustion amongst them, where a barrier of fatigue made it difficult for middle leaders to shift their understanding their role. Many were overburdened to the point of burnout.

At Bradbury School, senior leaders were learning how to shift their understanding of their roles as leaders beyond the hierarchies they had experienced, so that middle leaders could lead.

> For middle leaders, there is constant change and high pressure. You're dealing with student behaviour, your own work, everything else. Prioritising. Looking at what can be delegated. Being able to regulate your emotions. Some of our middle leaders are so dedicated. They do so many hours that it catches up with them sometimes and that's detrimental. Authentic support is needed. We need each other and it needs to be a relationship of respect and trust.
>
> I think there are still traditional hierarchies. From my experience, it's not until you understand what the executive role asks of you, that you can understand where the senior leadership team are coming from, and you can appreciate everything they do. Knowing each other's role beyond what's written in a role statement. Immersing yourself in that understanding and building that empathy.

Empathy was built through self-awareness and experience, which grew respect and trust. The first step the leaders took in understanding how to lead pedagogy together was shared awareness. The leaders then reflected on the practices that had changed between them:

> We are getting better at having shared conversations around the direction we are taking. Middle leaders share challenges or difficulties not for us to fix but as a collective sharing and problem-solving experience and it's been such a small thing to do, but it's fantastic because it's increased that sense of solidarity. We have changed our meeting structures away from transactional information meetings to listening sessions. We're breaking

up the sense that a meeting is where one person talks to you and tells you what to do. Middle leaders shape decisions about our philosophical understandings of assessment. Divergent views are now welcome because you need interesting solutions to the issues that we're having here. In turn, the teachers trust middle leaders. They feel that they can go and talk to them and sort things through. The biggest way that they can implement change is in knowing how each of their staff members in their care react to change.

Shared consensus through listening, not telling, was the start to leading pedagogy together at Bradbury.

Leading Pedagogy

Leading pedagogy at Bradbury involved department leaders and wellbeing leaders working separately. The senior leaders at Bradbury were aware of the siloing going on between learning and wellbeing:

> The learning component is sometimes seen as not connected to wellbeing. When push comes to shove the learning and administrative requirements take precedence.

There was a clear sense that the middle leaders lead learning, and this came through in their practices as well as valuing their role in the school strategy:

> Middle leaders are still at the coal face of teaching. They're implementing new curriculum and new pedagogical approaches themselves, and they are being given time to do their leadership role. We still don't have a culture of middle leaders feeling like they belong in the classrooms of their teams and that they can visit classrooms and offer that kind of pedagogical leadership. They're leaders of learning and pedagogy. They have one of the most important, if not the most important roles in school. They feed any change initiative and are at the forefront of what happens with students in classrooms as well as supporting staff. They ensure our strategic plan goes ahead. They create vision and excitement in their teams.

Middle leaders at Bradbury led pedagogical approaches, and this was kept separately from wellbeing in their understanding and in their practices.

Gifts

Understanding the contribution you can make as a leader from self-awareness of your gifts can drive your capacity to lead pedagogy. One middle leader reflects:

If there's a good teacher, schools recognise this and they'll say you could be a great middle leader but knowing and understanding the craft of teaching and learning and development of students and education and doing that in a holistic way, is very different from leading a team even though quality teaching and learning is foundational. Since completing my Bachelor of Education seven years ago, I have 'quickly' moved through stages of the profession: consistent casual teaching, term-long blocks, full-time temporary, full-time permanent, and coordinator roles. At each stage I have had a similar internal dialogue: Have I spent long enough in this phase of my career? Will I be able to manage the additional pressures and responsibilities? Why am I offered these opportunities over to some of my more experienced colleagues? Of course, these questions are not unique to me, but I think they lend themselves to a discussion about the practices associated with teaching and leading and the gifts required in leading pedagogy. The main thing is the passion. A strong mindset. A strong organisational skillset. Someone with a vision. People that lead by example, are strong role models themselves and take the time to work with the team closely and listen. The middle leaders that make the most significant changes have good relationships with staff, colleagues, students, and parents. Leading means working with people and maintaining effective relationships which may involve robust conversation, planning, and supporting teachers in thinking and building relationships beyond, smaller, academic groups or wellbeing spaces. They need to be good communicators. They link things back to quality teaching or best practice. They certainly need to know their curriculum content, but that's a given. The most important part is how they communicate and collaborate, making a cohesive team that can try new things and give feedback in a safe environment.

Just as middle leaders have distinct gifts in addition to excellence in teaching, an exceptional principal also had gifts in relationship building that went beyond any role description:

Our new Principal mentioned the other day, 'I feel like you can't leave one of these meetings feeling unhappy because no matter what goes down in those meetings, we finish off with a round of applause'. It sounds like something simple but it's that relationship building moment where we all look around the room and smile and have a laugh with each other. It's taken our team to the next level.

The simple practice of collective applause that involves not words of affirmation but rather a physical action where everyone participates builds the team through praise.

Connecting Research and Practice

Self-Awareness

Self-awareness is widely regarded as an important component of effective leadership (Carden et al., 2022). However, there is little consensus about what it is, how to measure it, and how to develop it. Some authors describe self-awareness as having two components: internal (or intrapersonal) self-awareness (knowing your own internal state, values, etc.) and external (or interpersonal) self-awareness (knowing how you appear to others) (Eurich, 2018; Carden et al., 2022).

A review paper suggests a model for understanding self-awareness as including both content and process (London et al., 2023). Content includes internal and external awareness, as above, and additional components such as self-identity. Process includes attention to the self (reflection, rumination, mindfulness) as well as self-knowledge (metacognition). This process component highlights that self-awareness is dynamic and changes over time – it requires constant development. However, we also need to be self-aware in a way that leads to positive outcomes. For example, when we reflect on a situation to learn from it ("What could I do differently in the future?"), this is quite different from ruminating on the same situation ("Why did I do that? I'm an idiot!"). Using techniques that allow us to distance ourselves from in-the-moment negative thoughts and feelings can be helpful in ensuring that we are reflecting rather than ruminating (Kross et al., 2023). Mindfulness, or attention to the current moment, gives us the ability to be self-aware while in a situation and adjust our responses (noticing that you are getting frustrated with a student for not paying attention, then realising that you haven't implemented accommodations for their ADHD today). Note that mindfulness in this sense is quite specific and is not synonymous with mindfulness meditation (although these practices can be used to hone this skill). Self-knowledge allows us to understand ourselves and adapt our behaviours and practices over time. ("I am too tired to have serious discussions in the afternoon; I will arrange those meetings for the morning.")

Some simple tools from psychology can help in gaining useful self-awareness skills that allow us to react intentionally in stressful situations. To use the process of reflection to gain a basic understanding of our reactions in a specific situation (i.e., internal and external self-awareness), we can use the cognitive-behavioural model. Note that the term behaviour here is not synonymous with behaviourism. It simply means observable actions in response to internal (thoughts, feelings, values, bodily sensations) or external stimuli and in this way is about practices. The following is an imaginary scenario which illustrates the steps in the model:

1. Specify the situation. For example, Stacey is a middle leader:
   I am concerned about the performance of Tom, a teacher in my team. Tom is a relatively new teacher in the team and is an early career teacher.

Looking at grades in Year 9 and 10, the students in Tom's class are not achieving as high grades as others in the cohort even though they are a mixed rather than graded cohort. I am also concerned there may be a classroom management issue. At times when I've walked down the corridor, I've noticed that students are really challenging Tom, I can hear loud noises and laughter and a sense of disrespect. In addition, everyone in my team is observed once a term, but whenever I try to schedule a date and time for a classroom observation Tom is quick to find a reason why this isn't possible.

2 Specify your thoughts, feelings, and behaviours in relation to this situation. It is helpful to think about behaviour in terms of approach and avoidance. When facing challenging situations, we may choose to avoid a situation because it brings up difficult thoughts or feelings, or we may choose to approach that situation to resolve it. For example, Stacey recognises the following:

> I have been putting off talking to Tom for months [avoidance behaviour] and would like to continue putting it off or involve one of the Executive team but I have decided I need to face this conversation [approach behaviour]. I am dreading it [feeling] and expect Tom will be upset and defensive [thoughts] as this is often his reaction in team meetings.
>
> I have struggled to connect with Tom like I do with other members of the team. My views on situations tend to be different and I have no idea of his life outside work. Tom has been particularly withdrawn and prickly lately.
>
> A small part of me realises that I have not tried to connect with Tom, and that I often respond negatively to his contributions in meetings [behaviours]. I feel guilty [feeling] that I have allowed this situation to continue for so long [thought], and this feeds into my reaction to him because talking to him reminds me of my avoidance of the issues [thoughts]. I also know that Tom's students like him and that he is particularly supportive of students with mental health issues.

In this example, Stacey is aware of her thoughts ("he'll be upset", "I'm avoiding the issue"), feelings (dread, guilt), and behaviour (avoiding a difficult situation, responding negatively in meetings, allowing a lack of personal connection to influence her treatment of a team member). She has decided to approach Tom about her concerns.

Let's look at this from the other side – what is Tom's perspective?

> I am an early career teacher and a relatively new teacher in the team. Stacey (my team leader) has asked for a meeting with me, and I have a bad feeling it is about my performance in the classroom. I am terrified [feeling] that I will eventually be found out and the school will realise my

teaching is not as good as others in the team [thought]. For this reason, I have been avoiding observations or any other changes [behaviour] that might make my poor performance visible (such as sharing assessments or coaching). I'm really enjoying [feeling] teaching Year 7 and Year 11 but am finding the Year 9 and 10 cohorts really challenging and I'm not sure why my strategies aren't working. I've been worried [feeling] about Jemima in Year 9 who is disruptive in class and I'm not sure how to find out more information about her or how to help her.

I have also noticed that Stacey doesn't seem to like me [thought] and rarely asks about my wellbeing. If I make a suggestion or complaint in team meetings she tends to shut it down. Because of this I haven't told her that my marriage has broken down lately and I am in a custody dispute with my spouse [behaviour]. This is making it hard to concentrate on work and I am aware that my teaching performance in the classroom has deteriorated. I love teaching [feeling] and am worried [feeling] that I will lose my job [thought] as my students are the positive part of my life.

A small part of me realises that avoiding observations and coaching [avoidance behaviour] means that I can't get help to improve my teaching, and I feel guilty [feeling] that I can't overcome this barrier to help my students [thoughts].

We can see in this example that Tom is in a more difficult situation than Stacey is aware of in both the personal (separation and custody issues) and professional (behaviour management issues and student concerns) realms. Like Stacey, he has been feeling worried and guilty and has been avoiding chances to resolve the situation.

The discussion between Stacey and Tom will have a different outcome based on how they approach this situation. The lack of relationship between the two of them makes it more likely there will be misunderstandings and a negative outcome. For example, if Stacey approaches the meeting assuming that Tom needs to be performance-managed, he will likely respond in a different way than if she approaches him with a desire to understand and support his teaching. Given his difficult personal situation, raising his anxiety level by the threat of consequences is unlikely to help him with his difficulties concentrating or his specific difficulties in knowing how to manage the class or help his student Jemima. Similarly, if Tom can harness his genuine love of teaching and his desire to help his students and is open to help rather than being immediately defensive, there is a better chance of a constructive outcome. The more each person can understand their own responses and take a broader perspective on the situation, the more likely they will be able to regulate their emotions and responses and stay focused on achieving the best outcome. The conversation between them will be more effective if they are both able to use mindfulness skills (i.e., awareness of their own responses in the moment) and distancing skills (stepping back from their own thought processes) as a process to regulate their responses.

There is another potential issue here about how observations and coaching are framed in the teaching team. Tom's behaviour in avoiding classroom observations may be affected by his beliefs about how these observations will be used – are they surveillance or a genuine attempt to help improve teaching and learning?

Stacey could reflect on questions such as "What is my intention in completing classroom observations?" "Do my practices reflect this intention?" and "How do my team perceive my intention?" Seeking feedback by gentle questioning about this from a perspective of curiosity may be a way for Stacey to understand Tom's views. For example, she could say something like "I've noticed that it's been hard to schedule a classroom observation with you. I'm wondering if you have any concerns about being observed?"

The final component of self-awareness relates to our identity and self-image, which includes our gifts. The following section supports educators to self-reflect on who they are as an educator and what they can bring to their school.

Pedagogical Gifts

We bring to the profession who we are. As Parker Palmer writes, 'we teach who we are' and 'we lead who we are' (Palmer, 1997). As one middle leader shared above, teachers are frequently promoted to school leadership positions because of their teaching prowess (Grootenboer, 2018). Role modelling is powerful, and expertise is important. Leading the child (pedagogy) and leading with others require understanding yourself as a teacher so you can lead pedagogy.

School leaders are first and foremost teachers. In England, principals are given the title 'Head Teacher', a title also given to middle leaders in some Australian secondary schools. In Western cultures (Wilkinson, 2022; Kemmis, 2022), leadership role titles have importance and school leadership tends to be more hierarchical. In northern Europe, there is less distinction between teachers and leaders in roles and practices, and educators lead pedagogy together (Wilkinson, 2022; Forssten Seiser 2020). Understanding yourself as a teacher is integral to understanding how you lead pedagogy with other colleagues. You can be an excellent teacher and administrator and not lead well with others. Leading pedagogy and wellbeing start with *me* because leading pedagogy begins with your self-awareness and your contribution and is best practised by *us* because leading together makes leading pedagogy possible.

Teachers who are committed to their vocation ask, *Who am I* as a teacher and what practices and arrangements support me to teach well and learn well? They also ask, *Who are my students and how do they learn*? and adjust their practice. Teaching well is connected to context, content knowledge, and the way that you understand your students and their learning. Crowther and Boyne (2016) call these combined practices your 'pedagogical gifts'. They argue that when you are teaching in your preferred context, in your area of expertise and passion, you will use your gifts well. For example, *Jill is best suited to teaching kindergarten in disadvantaged schools. She enjoys being hands-on. Jill's mum was a librarian, which taught Jill the wonder of literature. Jill sees her vocation as supporting kids' literacy skills so that they have a strong start in life.* In the gifts project, Crowther and Boyne (2016) encourage teachers to reflect upon theories of pedagogy and disciplinary knowledge that resonate with them the most, alongside unique aspects of their personality and character, to help teachers connect best with students and how teachers themselves like to learn. Crowther and Boyne (2016) asked numerous teachers to outline their gifts, supporting the development of school-wide pedagogies in schools. It is helpful if teachers and leaders understand self or '*me*' through their gifts, so that they can identify how they can contribute to the '*we*' of a team and a school.

The gifts project was borne out of the recognition that professional teaching standards could only ever be a universal baseline measure for teacher quality. Rather than basing teacher quality on baseline standards, enabling teachers to define their qualities more deeply through their identities and purpose may enable teachers to know themselves and value their contribution and commitment to the profession. We agree and take the perspective that teaching and leadership standards represent an outcome of good work but also do not provide teachers or leaders practices for working together.

Schools are communities, and yet teachers and school leaders are often working in isolation. Lortie's (1975) egg crate analogy illustrates this point, suggesting that teachers are like eggs working in individual classroom egg crates by themselves alongside each other. When leaders invite them to work together they may be walking on egg shells. Similarly, leaders working in offices on clearly defined roles are the same as eggs in egg crates. They cannot easily know students and how they learn, as exemplified in the Australian teaching standards because really knowing students and how they learn is a collective endeavour by all educators. When knowing students and how they learn becomes distanced from the practices of leading, for middle leaders, there can be a disconnect between what people do and how they see themselves. As one Senior Leader shared: "Our middle leaders here are exemplary administrators. They're highly organised, highly efficient … There's still a sense of helplessness from some of the middle leaders, like they don't know how to do the leadership dimension of their job." These leaders are preforming the role of bookkeeping student progress and attainment without connecting their role to their teaching identity or leading their team.

Teaching and leading together, or leading pedagogy together, is fundamental for the wellbeing of students and the workload and wellbeing of teachers and leaders. Interestingly, since Crowther and Boyne (2016) and Crowther, Addison, and Fox (2021) published their books about the hope of pedagogy and the importance of pedagogical balance and respect for the teaching profession in response to the development of professional teaching standards and the rising of anxiety in schools of both students and teachers, there has been a mass exodus from the teaching profession (Heffernan et al., 2022; Longmuir and McKay, 2024). Teachers and leaders perform administrative and relational pedagogical work. When people's work aligns with their gifts, values centred in learning relationships their wellbeing are enhanced. When educators and students draw upon each other's strengths, rather than fix weaknesses, wellbeing increases (Zeng et al., 2016). Understanding and valuing ourselves and others are valuable for our own wellbeing and the wellbeing of others. Understanding my pedagogical gifts involves connecting with my values and reflecting upon how they connect with the values of the school. This takes a stance of wondering, which has the potential to flow through to how we value students as individuals, with gifts and talents. If we know we are not all the same, we won't expect our students to all be the same. We encourage you to reflect upon your pedagogical gifts and to use Crowther and Boyne's resources to do so in practice.

Leading Pedagogy

Leading the child is every action between teachers and students and includes every purpose. We have intentionally chosen pedagogy as the most important term for leaders to understand in practice in leading the learning and wellbeing of students because pedagogy in Greek means to 'lead the child'. This section covers some key assumptions about pedagogy we need to consider carefully as we lead learning and wellbeing together.

First, the meaning of pedagogy is not universally understood (Grice et al., 2023; Forssten Seiser, 2021). Pedagogy has evolved over time across cultures and contexts today. The meaning of pedagogy can be about deep philosophical purpose or narrowed to teaching techniques, as it has been in Australian policy. Van Manen (1991) writes, "It is possible to learn all the techniques of instruction but to remain pedagogically unfit as a teacher" (p. 9). This means that pedagogy is about more than pedagogical approaches. Hence, second, pedagogy is not about teaching techniques (Grice, 2025). Leading children is a learning and a wellbeing responsibility, which means growing ourselves as educators and pedagogues and growing our students because "pedagogy is a fascination with the growth of the other" (Van Manen, 1991, p. 13) and their attainment.

Third, syllabus reform is not pedagogical reform (Grice, 2018). Syllabus reform may orient us away from having the time to know children and can lead teachers towards institutionalising them and us (Van Manen, 1991), decreasing our capacity to consider creative possibilities for students and ourselves. *Who I am* at its most personal becomes *who I am* as I teach and *who I am* as I lead and where leading pedagogy is reflective, cognitive, emotional, and about learning.

Fourth, if pedagogy means *leading the child*, pedagogy is about authentic relationships more than it is about system reform. It is both a philosophy of behaviour and a call for social justice, as critical pedagogues suggest.

Understanding pedagogy helps leaders to understand our purpose today as educators to build democracy through our interactions in schools. Riddle and Hickey (2024) note that decades of neoliberal school reform in Australia have "stultified and alienated young people from education" (p. 9) by abandoning the potential of relational pedagogy. Alexander (2008) reminds us to think beyond practice to the arrangements that enable pedagogy between learners:

> Pedagogy does not only refer to the act of teaching. It also includes all elements that inform, sustain, and justify teacher's actions, values, ideas, theories, beliefs, history and evidence as well as their relationship with the local and global context... making teaching an educative process rather than a merely technical one.
>
> (p. 210)

For this reason, fifth, we need to deeply understand our context and our students because pedagogy is about ourselves and our context, our gifts and their talents. It does not take teachers long to work out that teaching techniques cannot fully equip teachers for every pedagogical predicament (Van Manen, 1991, p. 195) because leading pedagogy involves understanding every student. Pedagogy brings us back to leading learning for and with the child at our school.

Sixth, pedagogy is an action and an agentic practice (Grice, 2025). Leading the child involves a never-ending series of micro-moments with children that we reflect upon and do as we teach and lead learning. American Kindergarten teacher and author Julie Diamond (2008) sums up the practice of pedagogy as "understanding children's thinking" done through "respect through shared authority and not control" (p. 67). She writes, "when teachers reflect together on the work of children, and children themselves, children become central to education" (p. 171). In this way, leading pedagogy is a *together* practice. Fundamental to the practice of pedagogy is agency, where "planning has as its goal children's development of the ability to govern themselves" (Diamond, 2008, pp. 28–29).

Pedagogical micro-moments of practice involve what Van Manen (1991) refers to as pedagogical tact. "Tact discerns what is unique and different about a child and attempts to enhance this uniqueness" (van Manen, 1991, p. 184). Research and empirical knowledge matter for understanding pedagogical moments, yet "the essence of pedagogy is neither. The pedagogical moment is the concrete and practical response to the question, 'What to do here?' Dealing with the child in the specific situation is the essence of pedagogy" (ibid, p. 44). Rather than pedagogy being technical or a "production enterprise" (ibid, p. 9), we need to consider its moral and human imperative. van Manen (1991) asserts that pedagogy cannot necessarily be "composed or studied" but rather "inspired".

Finally, in this way, pedagogy is hopeful. "Any relation between a parent or teacher with a child is always founded on hope." In embracing pedagogy for wellbeing through action pedagogy becomes political because it develops citizens who hope for the future:

A view of society that denies any of its citizens the opportunity to develop their fullest potential in relation to the rest of society is pedagogically corrupt. We should not, by means of our children, produce a world that we would not wish upon them. Pedagogy may thus become the impetus for political thought and action.

(Van Manen, 1991, pp. 211–212)

Pedagogy cannot be anything but authentic and responsible, guiding us and leading us through hope. It is tempting to avoid the word pedagogy, but if we do, we miss out on the very purpose of education and schooling for individuals and the collective and the integral connection between learning and wellbeing.

Understanding pedagogy may involve some instructing and coaching. Instructional leadership, alongside altruistic and idealistic views of pedagogy, should not lead to teachers feeling like they need to be perfect practitioners. The imperfection of teaching is authentically professional and part of what it means to be pedagogical:

Our efforts and desires to do the best we can (knowing that it is not always good enough) are still animated by pedagogical intent and by a sense of pedagogical responsibility …. freeing us to realize that it is impossible as pedagogues always to act right: to teach impeccable lessons, to be wise and fair, to explain difficult concepts with ease, always to keep the whole child in view, to be an inspiration to students, to understand perfectly a child's needs, to help students through deep learning difficulties.

(Van Manen, 1991, pp. 81–82)

Diamond writes about the practices of teaching Kindergarten and agrees: "We confront our limits and make whatever we can of our strengths. The central story is continuous, not heroic or definitive. In learning who children are, we learn who we are, as teachers and people" (Diamond, 2008, p. 6). Restoring the wellbeing of educators and students involves self-reflection, authenticity, empathy, and hope.

In practice, those who lead pedagogy practise awareness and observation through noticing and giving feedback. Feedback loops are an important part of leading pedagogy together. However, the way that observation and feedback are conducted will involve authentic communication and empathy, alongside noticing, collaborating, and not spying (Grice, 2019; Goldshaft, 2024).

Practice Menu

What we do is who we are. Knowing yourself and others involves practices of self-awareness, giving and receiving feedback, and action. The pedagogical gifts project can raise awareness of your strengths. The practice menu below invites leaders to reflect upon their current pedagogical and reflective practices to raise self-awareness and to gain clarity about leading practices.

Current practices	Questions about practice arrangements	Suggested practices for application
Sayings (communication) What do I say about pedagogy? Do I know what my pedagogical gifts are?	*Cultural-discursive arrangements* What does my school say about pedagogy? Can I share my pedagogical gifts with others, and help them identify theirs?	1 Using approaches for critical self-reflection to understand students and how they learn. 2 Reflect on view of pedagogy to understand what leading pedagogy means at our school for the wellbeing of students, teachers and leaders. 3 Develop self-awareness by reflecting upon your personal pedagogical gifts and listen to the gifts of colleagues and students. 4 Reflect on how you lead children in learning and wellbeing and how you know their strengths. 5 Consider observation and feedback loops that support critical self-reflection.
Doings Do I know what I'm good at? Am I using self-awareness skills to understand my own pedagogical practice? Am I authentic in my pedagogy and expecting imperfection? Am I leading beyond administration? Do I recognise gifts in students, teachers and leaders?	*Material-economic arrangements* Do we know what we are good at? Am I observing others and giving robust and empathetic feedback? Am I using critical self-reflection skills to help others reflect? Do we use these opportunities to evaluate our pedagogical practices? Are middle leaders encouraged to lead pedagogy beyond administration?	
Relatings Am I inspired by children and learning? Am I kind to myself? Do I reflect on what I enjoy about school and what drains me? Can I step back and reflect as well as use mindfulness to guide my actions? Do my strengths and pedagogical gifts help me to relate to others?	*Social-political arrangements* Are we inspired by children and learning? Do the critical self-reflection skills we use help us to understand my team better, and to help them feel heard? Do I exercise empathy with students and colleagues as we lead children together?	
Dispositions (habitus) Do I have a moral understanding of pedagogy that helps me to relate to students, colleagues and parents?	*Practice traditions* What kind of pedagogical leadership is there at our school? Do we observe each other and have opportunities to empathetically reflect on what we observed? How can I support leaders to develop pedagogy together?	

Summary of Key Points

- Self-awareness includes both intrapersonal and interpersonal awareness – knowing how we see ourselves and how others see us.
- Understanding your gifts builds self-awareness as a foundation for leading learning and wellbeing.
- Understanding the gifts of others supports others to lead beyond administration towards understanding and leading pedagogy (where administration may be part of the role but not its sole purpose).
- Pedagogy means to *lead the child*, and when leaders reflect on their individual gifts and recognise the gifts of colleagues and children, they lead.
- Appreciating our own gifts and the gifts of others strengthens wellbeing.
- Feedback loops through observation can help us be more authentic and empathetic in our practices as well as improve pedagogy.
- Connecting our gifts to the values and purposes of our school adds value and moral purpose.
- Children are the inspiration of education.

References

Alexander, R. (2008). *Essays on Pedagogy*. Oxon, UK: Routledge.

Carden, J., Jones, R.J., & Passmore, J. (2022). Defining self-awareness in the context of adult development: A systematic literature review. *Journal of Management Education*, 46(1), 140–177.

Crowther, F. Addison, B., & Fox, K. (2021). *Inspiring Hope: Personal Pedagogical Gifts in a World of Standards*. Victoria: Hawker Brownlow.

Crowther, F., & Boyne, K. (2016). *Energising Teaching: The Power of Your Unique Pedagogical Gift*. Victoria: ACER Press.

Diamond, J. (2008). *Kindergarten: A Teacher, Her Students, and a Year of Learning*. New York: The New Press.

Eurich, T. (2018). What self-awareness really is (and how to cultivate it). *Harvard Business Review*, 4(4), 1–9.

Forssten Seiser, A. (2020). Exploring enhanced pedagogical leadership: An action research study involving Swedish principals. *Educational Action Research*, 28(5), 791–806. DOI:10.1080/09650792.2019.1656661

Forssten Seiser, A. (2021). When the demand for educational research meet practice. *Research in Educational Administration and Leadership*, 6(2), 348–376. DOI:10.30828/real/2021.2.1

Goldshaft, B. (2024). *"They're Only Here to Observe". A Study of Observation-Grounded Mentoring Practices in Student Teachers' Practicum*. Doctoral dissertation. Skriftserien Oda.oslomet.no.

Grice, C. (2018). Leading pedagogical reform. *International Journal of Leadership in Education*, 22(3), 355–370. DOI:10.1080/13603124.2018.1463462

Grice, C. (2019). 007 Spies, surveillance and pedagogical middle leadership: For the good of the empire of education. *Journal of Educational Administration and History*, 51(2), 165–181. DOI:10.1080/00220620.2019.1583173

Grice, C. (2025). *The Practices of Leading Pedagogy*. Singapore: Springer.

Grice, C., Forssten Seiser, A., & Wilkinson, J. (2023). Decentring pedagogical leadership: Educational leading as a pedagogical practice. *Journal of Educational Administration and History*, 55(1), 89–107. DOI:10.1080/00220620.2022.2163381

Grootenboer, P. (2018). *The Practices of School Middle Leadership: Leading Professional Learning*. Singapore: Springer.

Heffernan, A., Bright, D., Kim, M., Longmuir, F., & Magyar, B. (2022). 'I cannot sustain the workload and the emotional toll': Reasons behind Australian teachers' intentions to leave the profession. *Australian Journal of Education*, 66(2), 196–209. DOI:10.1177/00049441221086654

Kemmis, S. (2022). *Transforming Practices: Changing the World with the Theory of Practice Architectures*. Singapore: Springer.

Kross, E., Ong, M., & Ayduk, O. (2023). Self-reflection at work: Why it matters and how to harness its potential and avoid its pitfalls. *Annual Review of Organizational Psychology and Organizational Behavior*, 10(1), 441–464.

London, M., Sessa, V.I., & Shelley, L.A. (2023). Developing self-awareness: Learning processes for self-and interpersonal growth. *Annual Review of Organizational Psychology and Organizational Behavior*, 10(1), 261–288.

Longmuir, F., & McKay, A. (2024). Teachers' workload strain: Considering the *density* as well as the quantity of teachers work. *Curriculum Perspectives*, 44, 561–565. DOI:10.1007/s41297-024-00279-2

Lortie, D. (1975). *Schoolteacher: A Sociological Study*. London: University of Chicago Press.

Murry, J.M. (1889–1957). Writings and personal papers of Katherine Mansfield. *Notebook 30 (1921)*. Wellington, New Zealand: Alexander Turnbull Library.

Palmer, P.J. (1997). *The Courage to Teach Exploring the Inner Landscape of a Teacher's Life*, San Francisco: Jossey-Bass Publishers.

Riddle, S., & Hickey, A. (2024). *Unlocking the Potential of Relational Pedagogy: Reimagining Teaching, Learning and Policy for Contemporary Schooling*. Oxon: Routledge.

van Manen, M. (1991). *The Tact of Teaching: The Meaning of Pedagogical Thoughtfulness*. New York: State University of New York Press.

Wilkinson, J. (2022). *Educational Leadership Through a Practice Lens*. Singapore: Springer.

Zeng, G., Hou, H., & Peng, K. (2016). Well-being of Chinese primary and middle school students: The mediating role of resilience. *Frontiers in Psychology*, 7: 1873. DOI:10.3389/fpsyg.2016.01873

3 What is Wellbeing and What Can You Do to Increase it?

Chapter 3 explores the topic of wellbeing in schools and particularly the neglected area of educator wellbeing. We discuss definitions of educator wellbeing and provide an overview of the research in this area. We outline the early stage of this research, highlighting the lack of agreement on concepts and methods, conflicting results, and limited evidence. We also introduce well-researched models of workplace stress and wellbeing from psychology and show how they apply to educators. Leading practices consistent with these models are provided for school leaders to consider. The evidence base for wellbeing interventions focusses almost exclusively on individual-level interventions (e.g., resilience or mindfulness training), neglecting workplace factors. Our book attempts the opposite – with a strong focus on team-level approaches that can be used by school leaders.

Examples in Schools

Maya Angelou famously said, "My mission in life is not merely to survive, but to thrive; and to do so with some passion, some compassion, some humor, and some style." Imagine if students *and* educators could flourish in their work in schools. The examples below illustrate schools where surviving and thriving are possible.

> It's hard to move people in terms of understanding their role and their influence in a school when they're seriously overburdened to the point of burnout

Negative wellbeing outcomes such as burnout have consequences for school improvement. One school we worked with was just coming out of COVID lockdowns, and many middle leaders in this school were feeling burnt out. There had been a change in leadership at the school, and although there was a drive for change and for middle leaders to take on new responsibilities, the executive team understood that this was going to take some time.

> If I see an issue and I want to make some change, usually I'll bring it up with the group. And everyone in that group is very supportive and are happy to look at changing things, adapting things for the betterment of the school or for the betterment of students or teachers or community members, whatever it is.

Positive wellbeing outcomes such as work engagement also have consequences for school improvement. Another school we worked with effectively distributed leadership amongst middle leaders by building a climate of psychological safety and empowering middle leaders to contribute to school decisions. The leadership team were working as a collective to improve their school.

Connecting Research and Practice

When thinking about wellbeing, we often focus on the absence of negative outcomes such as poor physical or mental health, burnout, and social isolation. While these are important to consider and are somewhat easier to define than wellbeing, they don't tell us the full story. Thriving as a human being is not about the absence of problems. These differences are highlighted in the case study examples above. In this chapter, we will outline how psychological theory and research helps us to understand wellbeing, particularly in the context of working as an educator.

> Being a leader of wellbeing means I am responsible for helping create a learning environment which promotes and provides for the physical, cognitive, and social and emotional growth of the school community. In the past, I read this role description through the lens of student wellbeing; however, I have begun to resituate my understanding: What about the rest of the community? What about the teachers?

The focus on social and emotional wellbeing in schools has been a welcome development over recent years, and there are many books and programs that focus on this area. Interventions have focused primarily on student wellbeing and show beneficial effects on a range of indicators, including academic performance and emotional wellbeing (Durlak et al., 2022). The Collaborative for Academic, Social, and Emotional Learning (CASEL) is a comprehensive source of information in this area (see https://casel.org).

It is only comparatively recently that a significant research base has been available on the drivers of teacher wellbeing, despite research showing that teacher and student wellbeing are connected (Maricuțoiu et al., 2023). It is this lesser-known area that will be the focus of this book and is an area where leaders can have a direct effect.

I notice that my teachers and staff often put on a *happy mask* around me, acting healthy and capable, trying hard to hide signs of tiredness or stress. Their real emotions only seem to surface when I am not around. How do I know this? Because I find myself doing the exact same thing with my own supervisor. It makes me wonder if, in a hierarchical culture like Vietnam, we feel the need to always appear strong to show our competence and worth at work, because we are afraid that showing vulnerability might cause our supervisors or colleague to doubt our ability. Sadly, even the school's workshops seem to imply that being strong or *resilient* means hiding our struggles at work rather than addressing them openly.

Our cultural context and views of wellbeing affect our practices in relation to it. In addition, the wellbeing of teachers affects their leadership practices (Ghamrawi et al., 2023), as can be seem in the example above.

What is Wellbeing?

There are many representations in the media about wellness, and these bear little resemblance to historical notions of wellbeing or to modern research and thinking on this subject. In addition, there are cross-cultural variations in how wellbeing is understood, such as whether wellbeing is seen as a predominantly individual or collective phenomenon (Liu et al., 2018). To understand what has influenced your ideas and to understand your own perspective, I encourage you to stop for a moment and reflect on what wellbeing means to you.

There are two key ideas in the scholarly literature on wellbeing. These ideas have a long history and date back to Aristotle's *Nicomachean Ethics*. They include hedonia and eudaemonia. Hedonia describes a high level of positive emotions, a low level of distress, and positive life satisfaction. We experience hedonia when we *feel good*. Eudaemonia refers to a person possessing "qualities that characterize an excellent human life, whether or not he or she happens to '*feel good*.' Eudaimonia is thus not conceived of as a mental state, a positive feeling, or a cognitive appraisal of satisfaction but rather as a way of living" (Ryan et al., 2008, p. 143). We experience eudaemonia when we are living a *good life*.

Hedonia and eudaemonia are sometimes referred to by the broader term "flourishing". These concepts help to remind us that the absence of a mental illness or of states such as burnout does not necessarily mean mental health. This view of wellbeing also means that everyone can experience it in their own way. You can have a chronic health condition, a disability, a mental health condition, or a terminal illness and still feel good at times and, perhaps more importantly, live a good life while you are here to your capacity.

What do we Know About Educator Wellbeing?

> Every school is feeling it across the board and industry, that whole notion of quiet quitting… they're feeling burnt out.

Overall, we know more about negative than positive wellbeing outcomes for educators. For example, over 50% of Australian educators are very or extremely stressed, especially early career teachers, primary teachers, and teachers working in rural and remote areas (Carroll et al., 2022). Sources of stress include workload, student behaviour, and unrealistic expectations (Collie, 2023) and complex learning, behaviour and social needs of students, increasing burden of administration and data collection, limited support from school and system leadership, and an overloaded curriculum (Longmuir et al., 2022).

It is only very recently that we have some major published reviews of educator wellbeing. The first was by McCallum and colleagues in 2017 and provided a useful starting point for thinking about this issue.

> Wellbeing is diverse and fluid respecting individual, family and community beliefs, values, experiences, culture, opportunities and contexts across time and change. It is something we all aim for, underpinned by positive notions, yet is unique to each of us and provides us with a sense of who we are which needs to be respected.
> (McCallum et al., 2017, p. 17)

This quote is important as it illustrates the diversity of individual circumstances and how these relate to wellbeing, but it doesn't tell us what wellbeing is or isn't.

Hascher and Waber (2021) conducted a systematic review of 20 years of the qualitative and quantitative empirical literature on teacher wellbeing and concluded that there was no consensus on the definition of teacher wellbeing. They further concluded that almost everything correlates with teacher wellbeing in the available research, which doesn't provide clear guidance about the major risk factors. Note that Hascher and Waber were essentially looking at the antecedents of teacher wellbeing rather than wellbeing itself. In this case, antecedents refer to those things that come before teacher wellbeing in a temporal sense – they may or may not be causal, and we are unlikely to know anytime soon. In addition, as wellbeing is so individual and based on context, this may be impossible!

Zhou et al. (2024), in a meta-analysis of the quantitative literature on the antecedents of teacher wellbeing, also concluded that most variables measured contributed to teacher wellbeing. They highlighted that wellbeing itself was measured in many different ways and that many of these work as proxies for wellbeing (e.g., measures of work engagement). Both Hascher and Waber (2021) and Zhou et al. (2024) concluded that the social determinants of workplace wellbeing seem particularly important for educators.

In response to the state of the research on teacher wellbeing, the OECD (Organisation for Economic Co-operation and Development) commissioned a paper to develop a framework for data collection on teacher wellbeing (Viac & Fraser, 2020). This framework includes both antecedents and consequences of teacher wellbeing and a definition of wellbeing. Teacher wellbeing in this model has four components: cognitive wellbeing, subjective wellbeing, physical and mental wellbeing, and social wellbeing. The antecedents include educational system factors, the working environment (demands and resources), and school and teacher characteristics. The consequences include "inward" outcomes (e.g., burnout) and "outward" outcomes (e.g., classroom processes and student wellbeing).

The recent increase in research on teacher wellbeing is a positive development, but there is a lot we don't know and a lot of theoretical development yet to occur. The research suggests that context and the social aspects of school environments are extremely important. Despite the early stage of this research, there is ample research on workplace wellbeing in general and much of this can be straightforwardly applied to educator wellbeing.

Psychosocial Hazards

The literature on occupational stress is extensive, and we know a lot about the risk factors for workplace injury claims. Psychosocial hazards are the workplace factors that contribute to individual harms such as mental and physical health concerns. Knowledge about the impact of psychosocial hazards in workplaces is so well established that it is increasingly recognised in workplace health and safety legislation and in international standards such as ISO 45003:2021. Research in 2019 found that 29 percent of 132 countries examined had legislative requirements around psychosocial hazards and mental health in the workplace, and this percentage rose to 82 percent of developed countries in the European Union (Chirico et al., 2019). Since then, regulations have also been introduced in Australia, and there are calls for similar regulatory frameworks in the United States (Schulte et al., 2024).

In practice, this requires that organisations assess whether known psychological hazards translate to actual risks in their context. For example, exposure to traumatic events is unlikely in your standard office job but is a definite risk in emergency services. The following example is from a middle leader in a school:

> My first two-point leadership position came in the form of a wellbeing role after seven years of teaching and a year into a move to a new school. On a macro level I contributed to the policies and frameworks that target the wellbeing needs of students across the school, while my day-to-day practices involved seeing to the needs of a cohort of students within my designated pastoral care house group. This spanned from critical child protection matters to monitoring behaviour. I found the jump to this

role was hard to prepare for seeing as wellbeing matters are traditionally cordoned off to protect student privacy. Straight away I was launched into a whole new world - in my first week I was liaising with a family whose daughter attempted to take their own life. I was asked to manage this move with very little onboarding, both in terms of policy and procedures, and professional development in managing a team. It was implied that I would 'pick it up as I go.' I quickly came to question whether this was the most effective way of nurturing someone new to middle leadership. There were psychological hazards littered throughout my work and I had very little technical expertise to draw on. It seemed nonsensical to teach Year 9s about Romeo and Juliet after, five minutes before, helping a student bandage their self-harm wounds. I planned to nominate myself for wellbeing and leadership-specific professional development to help with the process, however the demands of the role saw it slip to the bottom of my priority list. In the end I had to draw on and refine my own mental health practices outside of work.

This example highlights a number of psychosocial hazards. Drawing on the regulatory framework in place where this educator works (*Code of Practice: Managing Psychosocial Hazards at Work*, 2021), we can see "role overload" (frequent exposure to distressing events, critical incidents where their decisions may have safety impacts on students), exposure to traumatic events (suicide and self-harm), role conflict (bandaging wounds and then teaching Shakespeare), lack of role clarity (insufficient training), and poor support from management ("pick it up as I go"). We can also see the impact of these hazards on a dedicated teacher who, owing to work demands, was unable to complete the professional development training they needed and had to make additional efforts to maintain their own mental health outside work.

The Job Demands-Resources Model

The Job Demands-Resources (JD-R) model is a long-standing and well-researched model from the occupational stress literature (Bakker et al., 2023). It seeks to explain the drivers of both negative (health impairment) and positive (motivational) workplace outcomes. The key idea behind the JD-R model is that both job demands and job resources have important consequences for wellbeing and hence performance, and resources have the strongest relationship to positive outcomes (Bakker et al., 2023).

Demands in the model fall into two categories: challenges and hindrances (Van den Broeck et al., 2010). Challenges are tasks or experiences we find interesting or meaningful or stretch our skills. These are generally beneficial to us as long as we have the time available to do them and not too many other things on our plate. That is, as long as we have the resources to do them. For example, this might include relatively small tasks such as building a new lesson plan based on a new idea you've had for engaging students and larger tasks such as taking on a new leadership role. The research evidence shows that challenge demands increase work engagement and have favourable long-term effects on wellbeing and performance (Bakker et al., 2023). Hindrance demands are work tasks that drain us and impair our functioning; that is, they hinder us in our work (Van den Broeck et al., 2010). This can include relatively simple but frustrating experiences such as having to enter the same data twice into different systems. These types of demands have negative long-term effects on wellbeing.

Resources include the psychosocial, physical, and organisational aspects of work that motivate us, help us to meet goals, mitigate the effects of job demands, and help us develop (Bakker et al., 2023). Workplace resources could include physical infrastructure such as buildings or IT, social resources such as supportive colleagues, good leadership, access to information, and skills and training. The model includes personal resources such as self-efficacy, optimism, and self-esteem (Bakker et al., 2023).

Reasonable job demands combined with sufficient job resources are what make work sustainable in the long term. This makes intuitive sense, but rarely do we analyse our work in a systematic way. People will often see their inability to complete work as a personal flaw – we think we need to be more organised, work faster, be more focused, procrastinate less, find more time for work, and so on. Instead, it is useful to break this down systematically by digging into the nature of different demands and resources.

Negative Wellbeing Outcomes

There are a variety of possible negative wellbeing outcomes of unsustainable or toxic work environments. Some that are relevant to educators include poor physical and mental health and burnout.

Poor Physical and Mental Health

The psychosocial hazards described earlier in this chapter can lead to, or exacerbate, mental health problems such as anxiety, depression, or post-traumatic stress disorder (Schulte et al., 2024). They can also lead to, or exacerbate, physical health problems such as cardiovascular disease, migraine headache, obesity, and high blood pressure (Schulte et al., 2024). They may also lead to experiences such as moral injury (Sugrue, 2020), compassion fatigue, and secondary traumatic stress (Ormiston et al., 2022).

Burnout

There is ample evidence that teachers worldwide are experiencing high levels of burnout, leading to many educators leaving the profession (Madigan & Kim, 2021). As discussed above, high work demands and inadequate resources can lead to burnout. For example, the demands of a challenging classroom cohort, combined with inadequate training in classroom management and trauma-informed teaching and lack of in-classroom support can lead to burnout. Similarly, increasing administrative demands or curriculum crowding without an increase in resources can, over time, lead to exhaustion and burnout.

Burnout was first included in the 11th Revision of the International Classification of Diseases (ICD-11) in May 2019 as an occupational phenomenon. The World Health Organization (2022) defines burnout as "a syndrome conceptualized as resulting from chronic workplace stress that has not been successfully managed". It is *not* classified as a medical condition. It is important to note that the stress must be chronic (not intermittent or short-term) and that successful management of stress requires action by both workplaces and individuals.

> At this point of time in my career, I feel increasingly overwhelmed with the amount of information I am trying to process. The many roles and responsibilities and the high expectations for my role as AP cause me to doubt my abilities as a professional. We constantly talk about "doing less better" but this seems impossible. In recent years I struggled to be a full-time classroom teacher and an AP leading a team of 8-9 staff.

Burnout has three components which can be clearly seen in the quote above. The first is *emotional exhaustion* which persists over time (World Health Organization, 2022). These feelings of exhaustion can also affect our ability to self-regulate effectively as we struggle to sleep, exercise, or otherwise recover from work. It is also common for people to become irritable or avoidant as their stress levels increase and their fatigue increases. This state can be seen in the above quote: "I feel increasingly overwhelmed". We can recover from this component of burnout if we address it early and before it leads to the other components of burnout.

The second component of burnout is *a reduced sense of professional efficacy* (World Health Organization, 2022). We start to doubt the quality of our work or even whether we are suited to this type of work at all. Early career educators may be especially at risk here because of their lack of experience. Doubting ourselves can also stem from inadequate resources to meet demands which we may not identify as the true reason behind our doubts. Similarly, working in a highly critical environment puts us at risk as we lack the resources provided by supportive leadership and team climate. In the quote above, this is illustrated by work demands which "cause me to doubt my abilities as a professional". Again, this aspect of burnout can be addressed by access to appropriate support if identified early.

The final component of burnout is *cynicism about work or a sense of increased mental distance from work* (World Health Organization, 2022). For example, a teacher may start to feel that the whole education system is broken or that their particular school is dysfunctional. In the quote above, this is seen in the following: "We constantly talk about "doing less better" but this seems impossible". Again, if identified early, this can be addressed.

All these factors are warning signs that we do well to heed if we want to sustain fulfilling careers in our chosen professions. Recovery from full burnout (where we have more than one of the above symptoms and they have been going on for some time) is difficult and may require major changes to our working lives. There is also the risk that burnout will lead to or exacerbate existing mental health issues.

Work Engagement

Where there is a good balance between work demands and resources, we may instead experience the positive mental state of work engagement which includes vigor, dedication and absorption.

> Vigor refers to high levels of energy and mental resilience while working, the willingness to invest effort in one's work, and persistence even in the face of difficulties. Dedication implies being strongly involved in one's work and experiencing a sense of significance, enthusiasm, and challenge. Absorption refers to being fully concentrated and happily engrossed in one's work, whereby time passes quickly
>
> (Bakker et al., 2023, p. 27).

The first two qualities can be clearly seen in the quote below:

> And as one of the leaders, I have no intentions of going anywhere, I love this school, I love this place. I'm just so excited to see what happens with the team next, especially at the end of this year we build our new plan and I know that everything that you have taught us and we worked on, we're actually going to be putting that into action within that plan as well. And that's something really exciting.

Both Processes can be Occurring at Once

It is important to note that we can experience the early stages of burnout while experiencing work engagement. As Amra Pajalic (2023) writes:

> I love entering the classroom and being present in the moment with my students as we do an unspoken dance together and I gauge their energy and enthusiasm, pivoting my lesson plan to capture their attention.

I love the moments when I see them sparkle as they learn something, and the way that I see a concept anew through their eyes.

The classroom is my happy place, and my students are the fuel to my fire, but I also recognise that I am not the same teacher as I was in 2018....

I am burdened with busy work, and assessments are piling up more and more. Meanwhile students emotional needs are higher, requiring more finesse and care, and I am one of the teachers at risk of suffering emotional burnout as I am split between all these demands....

It's a battle that is fought within schools by all teachers, and it is a battle I fight every year, to bring myself back from the brink of burnout and find joy with my students to keep teaching.

The experience of the emotional exhaustion component of burnout is clearly present here in "I am burdened...I am split", but there is also a clear sense of work engagement. We can see vigor in "my students are the fuel to my fire", dedication in "pivoting my lesson plan to capture their attention", and absorption in "being present in the moment with my students as we do an unspoken dance together".

Wellbeing Interventions

Workplace wellbeing interventions are not well researched overall, and there is little specific research on interventions to address educator wellbeing. Overall, the majority of interventions are individual-level interventions rather than workplace ones (Rugulies et al., 2023). This is despite clear evidence that these interventions are generally not effective in improving worker wellbeing (Fleming, 2024) and may be a means of silencing workers (Murphy & MacMahon, 2022). It is also easier to send people to a training course than to change workplace structures and culture. It is not, however, necessarily more effective, as is shown by the limited evidence for the effectiveness of these interventions.

We should also ask: is it reasonable to expect that every educator should be mentally and physically well, have stable finances and housing, not have experienced (or be experiencing) any trauma, and have no demands outside work? Telling a parent with young children, an older woman going through menopause while caring for elderly parents, or someone with a chronic health condition or a complex trauma history that they need to "be resilient" is not a helpful response.

A further difficulty is that wellbeing interventions often lack what psychologists call "face validity" in that educators can easily see that an intervention is not related to their real work problems. They are often imposed rather than being based on an identified need, can be perceived as allowing organisations to tick a box, and can trivialise the real problems that people are facing. Consider the response of someone facing domestic or family violence on attending a typical "stress management" seminar at work. Providing these types of wellbeing interventions can, at their worst, send an implicit (or explicit?) message that the problem is located in the individual, not the workplace.

Leading in Practice

Active Listening

While measurement tools are available (see Practice Tips), one simple way to understand the wellbeing of those you work with is to use active listening skills. Very few people are explicitly taught these skills unless they are from specific professions such as psychologists, social workers, or counsellors. Some people pick them up in other ways, but they require such a different intention to our normal way of conversing that we often don't make the switch when it would be helpful. However, if we're lucky, we have experienced the effects of active listening. Take a moment to think about someone you know who has helped you to feel heard – what is it that they say or do? What effect has this had on you?

There are a few basic components of active listening that can be learnt with practice, including listening to understand, reflecting and clarifying, and asking open-ended questions.

Listening to Understand Rather Than Listening to Respond

During everyday life, we are often asked questions to which we need to respond. (Think about how many times a day a young child says "Mummy, can I...?") Educators and leaders have often described to us the pressure to "fix" things for either their students or team – often they are busy and want to "fix" things as quickly as possible. This pressure can get in the way of listening or asking questions that would allow a different type of response. It is worthwhile to ask ourselves, do we want other people to fix things for us, or would we rather be supported to work it out for ourselves?

An alternative is to listen to understand – to listen, really listen, and not be thinking about what you will say next. This requires being present for the other person and not caught up in our own thoughts. This can be hard to do and requires practice and intention.

Reflecting Back What was Said and Clarifying

This involves two related components: one is stating a quick summary of what you have heard the other person say (without adding your own ideas). This is an important step in helping the other person to feel heard. Think about how frustrating it is to explain something to another person and have them respond in a way that shows they haven't heard a word you've said. Another important skill in clear communication is to check your understanding – this is asking something simple like "Did I get that right?" This gives them a chance to correct any misunderstanding. Sometimes this simple step of reflecting and clarifying is enough to help people understand their own situation.

For example:

> I hear you have some concerns about the new curriculum, particularly about multidisciplinary collaboration and how that is going to work given how busy the team is already, but also about the impact of new lesson planning. Have I got that right?

Asking Questions to Enhance Understanding

There are particular types of questions that aid understanding. In particular, it is best to focus on open-ended questions. Open-ended questions are phrased to generate an expanded response rather than a yes/no ("Do you want ice cream?") or categorical ("What flavour would you like?) answer. These questions are particularly important in understanding other perspectives rather than making assumptions. For example, if we were wanting to understand the wellbeing of a colleague from the perspective of JD-R Theory, we could ask "What energises you at work?" (challenge demands and resources) and "What drains you at work?" (hindrance demands). Sometimes people will still provide a vague or brief response to an open-ended question. We can often encourage a more thoughtful or detailed response by adding a probing or clarifying question. These can be either a question ("Could you tell me more about it?" or "Can you give an example?") or a statement ("Tell me more about…").

Here is an imaginary scenario illustrating the power of an elaborated response, using Sam (a middle leader) and Alex (a classroom teacher):

Sam: What energises you most at work? [OPEN-ENDED QUESTION]
Alex: Definitely lesson planning.
Sam: What do you like about lesson planning? [CLARIFYING QUESTION]
Alex: I like the creativity of it – coming up with ideas and thinking about what will engage students. It reminds me of what I love about my

	subject area, and some time to explore what is happening in my field. I also like that it gives me some time out.
Sam:	You mentioned some time out, can you tell me more about that? [CLARIFYING QUESTION]
Alex:	I find teaching exhausting sometimes, the noise and the competing demands for my attention and student behaviour. Lesson planning is some quiet recovery time.
Sam:	Are there any particular classes that are more challenging? [CLARIFYING QUESTION]
Alex:	Definitely. Year 9 is the hardest the students are just not engaged and I find them hard to manage. I've tried everything I can think of and I can't work out what to do. It really makes me doubt myself and my teaching skills. If it wasn't for my Year 10 students I don't think I could keep going. At least when I'm doing my lesson plan I feel like I'm working toward a solution.
Sam:	What is different in the Year 10 class? [CLARIFYING QUESTION]
Alex:	I just feel more connected to the students. They're interested in the subject and we have great conversations – I feel like I can be more creative in responding to them because my mood is better, and I feel calmer. I can give them more of a say in what we do, whereas in Year 9 I am focused on trying to control the class and I feel stressed all the time.
Sam:	So, if I'm hearing you correctly your Year 10 classes are less draining because there are better relationships, more engagement, and you are calmer and interact differently with the students. But in Year 9 the classroom is more disrupted, students are less engaged and because you're stressed you interact differently with them as well. Have I got that right? [REFLECTION]
Alex:	Yes, exactly! I hadn't put it together before though that my stress levels are also affecting how I am with the students. I wonder if… [SELF REFLECTION]

At the end of this brief conversation, we can see that both Sam and Alex have a better understanding of Alex's workplace wellbeing. They are now both aware that a specific problem in teaching Year 9 is contributing to Alex experiencing some symptoms of burnout (exhaustion and professional self-doubt). We can also see that in a different context (Year 10 and when lesson planning) Alex is experiencing work engagement. Towards the end of the conversation, we can also see that Alex's wellbeing is affecting his teaching and that the conversation is helping Alex to self-reflect. This new understanding opens a door to solving the problem and may ultimately improve teaching and learning in the Year 9 classroom.

Practice Menu

Current practices	Questions about broader arrangements	Suggested practices for application
Sayings What do people say about wellbeing? What do people say about wellbeing programs? **Doings** Do leaders take action on psychosocial hazards? Do leaders support people with mental health concerns? **Relatings** Do people support each other's wellbeing? How do people respond when a colleague is struggling? **Dispositions** Is there stigma around mental health? Do people believe wellbeing is important? Is there a compassionate view of mental health?	When and how is wellbeing discussed if at all? Are there formal systems for identifying and managing psychosocial hazards? Are there formal systems for measuring educator wellbeing? Is time allocated for discussions of educator wellbeing? Is educator wellbeing embedded in discussions about school improvement? Are there formal workplace wellbeing programs? Are leaders trained to support wellbeing? Is training available on the social causes of poor wellbeing and how to address them? Do people use any wellbeing programs that are provided? How do leaders typically respond to mental health and wellbeing concerns?	- Assessing educator wellbeing in your school using formal measures such as - A broad wellbeing measure such as the Utrecht Work Engagement Scale (Schaufeli & Bakker, 2004) available online at https://www.wilmarschaufeli.nl/publications/Schaufeli/Test%20Manuals/ - Surveys assessing psychosocial hazards such as the People at Work Survey available online at (https://www.peopleatwork.gov.au/webcopy/healthhazards). - Assessing and addressing wellbeing in your school using active listening skills to understand educator's lived experience of wellbeing at school. - Actively addressing workplace drivers of poor wellbeing. - Placing more emphasis on building work engagement.

> **Summary of Key Points**
>
> - A focus on individual interventions is inadequate in addressing the drivers of poor mental health and burnout as well as low levels of wellbeing in organisations.
> - Measures of work engagement seem to be reasonable proxies for teacher wellbeing. It would be reasonable to use these concepts as an estimate of wellbeing in a school or workplace.

- Given the limits of the research on antecedents of teacher wellbeing, it would be reasonable to use known psychosocial hazards as a starting point and then add to or subtract from the list based on risks in the specific school context.
- School context seems to be an important variable to consider, given the heterogeneity in findings.
- Finally, if you want to know what is affecting wellbeing in your context, the simplest thing to do is ask! However, for teachers to use their voice requires a climate of psychological safety. Active listening can help in understanding what is affecting wellbeing in your school.
- It is a good idea to start by reflecting on your own wellbeing. This can be one using the measurement tools discussed below or by using the self-reflective processes discussed in the previous chapter.

References

Bakker, A.B., Demerouti, E., & Sanz-Vergel, A. (2023). Job demands–resources theory: Ten years later. *Annual Review of Organizational Psychology and Organizational Behavior*, 10(1), 25–53.

Carroll, A., Forrest, K., Sanders-O'Connor, E., Flynn, L., Bower, J.M., Fynes-Clinton, S., York, A., & Ziaei, M. (2022). Teacher stress and burnout in Australia: Examining the role of intrapersonal and environmental factors. *Social Psychology of Education*, 25(2), 441–469.

Chirico, F., Heponiemi, T., Pavlova, M., Zaffina, S., & Magnavita, N. (2019). Psychosocial risk prevention in a global occupational health perspective. A descriptive analysis. *International Journal of Environmental Research and Public Health*, 16(14), 2470.

Code of Practice: Managing Psychosocial Hazards at Work. (2021). Lisarow NSW: NSW Government.

Collie, R.J. (2023). Teacher well-being and turnover intentions: Investigating the roles of job resources and job demands. *British Journal of Educational Psychology*, 93(3), 712–726.

Durlak, J.A., Mahoney, J.L., & Boyle, A.E. (2022). What we know, and what we need to find out about universal, school-based social and emotional learning programs for children and adolescents: A review of meta-analyses and directions for future research. *Psychological Bulletin*, 148(11–12), 765.

Fleming, W.J. (2024). Employee well-being outcomes from individual-level mental health interventions: Cross-sectional evidence from the United Kingdom. *Industrial Relations Journal*, 55(2), 162–182.

Ghamrawi, N., Naccache, H., & Shal, T. (2023). Teacher leadership and teacher wellbeing: Any relationship? *International Journal of Educational Research*, 122, 102261.

Hascher, T., & Waber, J. (2021). Teacher well-being: A systematic review of the research literature from the year 2000–2019. *Educational Research Review*, 34, 100411.

Liu, L.B., Song, H., & Miao, P. (2018). Navigating individual and collective notions of teacher wellbeing as a complex phenomenon shaped by national context. *Compare: A Journal of Comparative and International Education*, 48(1), 128–146.

Longmuir, F., Cordoba, B.G., Phillips, M., Allen, K.-A., & Moharami, M. (2022). *Australian Teachers' Perceptions of Their Work in 2022.*

Madigan, D.J., & Kim, L.E. (2021). Towards an understanding of teacher attrition: A meta-analysis of burnout, job satisfaction, and teachers' intentions to quit. *Teaching and Teacher Education, 105*, 103425.

Maricuțoiu, L., Pap, Z., Ștefancu, E., Mladenovici, V., Valache, D.G., Popescu, B.D., Ilie, M., & Vîrgă, D. (2023). Is teachers' well-being associated with students' school experience? A meta-analysis of cross-sectional evidence. *Educational Psychology Review, 35*(1), 1.

McCallum, F., Price, D., Graham, A., & Morrison, A. (2017). *Teacher Wellbeing: A Review of the Literature.* Sydney: Association of Independent Schools of New South Wales.

Murphy, C., & MacMahon, J. (2022). Employee resilience: A labour process perspective. *Work in the Global Economy, 2*(1), 109–131.

Ormiston, H.E., Nygaard, M.A., & Apgar, S. (2022). A systematic review of secondary traumatic stress and compassion fatigue in teachers. *School Mental Health, 14*(4), 802–817.

Pajalic, A. (2023). I'm a teacher fighting burnout, but my students keep me energised. *ABC Education.* https://www.abc.net.au/education/i-am-fighting-teacher-burnout-but-my-students-keep-me-energised/102707710

Rugulies, R., Aust, B., Greiner, B.A., Arensman, E., Kawakami, N., LaMontagne, A.D., & Madsen, I.E. (2023). Work-related causes of mental health conditions and interventions for their improvement in workplaces. *The Lancet, 402*(10410), 1368–1381.

Ryan, R. M., Huta, V., & Deci, E. L. (2008). Living well: A self-determination theory perspective on eudaimonia. *Journal of Happiness Studies, 9*(1), 139–170.

Schaufeli, W., & Bakker, A. (2004). UWES Utrecht Work Engagement Scale Preliminary Manual. Utrecht: Occupational Health Psychology Unit Utrecht University.

Schulte, P.A., Sauter, S.L., Pandalai, S.P., Tiesman, H.M., Chosewood, L.C., Cunningham, T.R., Wurzelbacher, S.J., Pana-Cryan, R., Swanson, N.G., & Chang, C.C. (2024). An urgent call to address work-related psychosocial hazards and improve worker well-being. *American Journal of Industrial Medicine, 67*(6), 499–514.

Sugrue, E. P. (2020). Moral injury among professionals in K–12 education. *American Educational Research Journal, 57*(1), 43–68.

Van den Broeck, A., De Cuyper, N., De Witte, H., & Vansteenkiste, M. (2010). Not all job demands are equal: Differentiating job hindrances and job challenges in the job demands–Resources model. *European Journal of Work and Organizational Psychology, 19*(6), 735–759.

Viac, C., & Fraser, P. (2020). Teachers' well-being: A framework for data collection and analysis. *OECD Education Working Papers No. 213.* DOI:10.1787/19939019

World Health Organization. (2022). *ICD-11: International Classification of Diseases (11th Revision).* https://icd.who.int/

Zhou, S., Slemp, G. R., & Vella-Brodrick, D. A. (2024). Factors associated with teacher wellbeing: a meta-analysis. *Educational Psychology Review, 36*(2), 63. DOI:10.1007/s10648-024-09886-x

4 Trust and Psychological Safety

How brave do you think it is to trust people in schools today? Trust can be an intangible term. We live in an era of accountability and suspicion, verification, and transparency. Chapter 4 introduces the importance of trust in schools and the positive impact that trust has on learning, working together, and school improvement. A climate of trust is where leaders trust teachers and teachers trust leaders. Ultimately, trust involves making generous assumptions about the intentions of others and verifying these through action. Trust and psychological safety are bound up together in our assumptions of others. Psychological safety refers specifically to whether people can use their voice in the school environment – to ask questions, raise problems, make suggestions, and admit to mistakes. Psychological safety is foundational to wellbeing and performance in dynamic environments where there is a commitment to excellence. This chapter will encourage leaders to reflect on trust and psychological safety in their school and develop leadership practices that encourage voice and support trust and psychological safety.

Examples from Schools

Trust begins with someone demonstrating generous assumptions of others. That someone might be you, teaching in a classroom, choosing to trust your students, or you as a leader, choosing to trust your team. This may be built over time through accountability and verification. We know that learning and working together involve trust. Sometimes people make mistakes, and in climates of trust they can be transparent, and people can come up with new solutions together.

Paulo Freire (1970) illustrated the reciprocal nature of trust when he wrote "The trust of the people in the leaders reflects the confidence of the leaders in the people." As Paulo Freire reminds us, trust between people and leaders is like a mirror. You can see trust reflected in how they see each other. Leaders should demonstrate confidence in their people first, as they lead trust. The three scenarios below demonstrate what trust-building can look like in different schools as it is reflected and mirrored between school leaders and teachers.

62 *Leading Learning and Wellbeing Together*

The practices of trust either enable or constrain the work people do together. The metaphor of the mirror can help people to see more clearly what trust looks like.

Ana Morphosis School: Remodelling a Distorted Image

In a mirror, you see a reversed image of yourself. The image can be distorted. Using the mirror metaphor, one school we will refer to as Ana Morphosis School was embarking on an enabling leadership project for their middle leaders. Middle leaders would be taking on more responsibility in the school. This was a substantial change to the school. Previously, a highly respected principal had led a smooth-running hierarchical school where all decisions passed through their office. They were known to be a benevolent dictator. This high level of control constrained the development of leadership skills in others because there was minimal expectation that middle leaders could or would lead. Middle leaders were seen as administrators or managers, not leaders. This approach to middle leadership would struggle to satisfy curriculum, teaching, and assessment requirements today, given the expectation that all teachers know students and how they learn and the high expectations on teacher quality and accountability. When the new principal was appointed, the lack of confidence that middle leaders had in themselves was mirrored by a lack of confidence that the new principal had in them to lead. The new principal recognized that they needed skill development alongside permission to lead.

Some middle leaders did not desire this for themselves, whilst others craved the opportunity to develop. Middle leaders had a distorted image of their capacity, as did senior leaders, where their own perceptions impacted the level of trust between them, and the principal. No one knew quite how to look into the mirror. A senior leader admitted: "We haven't created the opportunities for them to – to really lead with confidence". This changed as the school moved from a culture of no trust to a culture of information-sharing and devolvement of responsibility, where middle leaders were trusted to lead. As one senior leader shared:

> There wasn't trust. There wasn't valuing… it was a culture of just tell me what to do and I'll do it. The middle leaders not feeling they had a voice. Not being in regular meetings, not feeling that they were part of the direction. It's a significant shift. A different way of doing things. I'd call it a cultural shift.

The senior leadership changed meeting practices which reflected a change in the mirror of trust. The executive changed the meeting structure away from "meetings for meetings' sake" and enabled the middle leaders' "voice" and practised "listening and hearing and responding by getting them to verbalise what they need so that they've got some level of trust to look after their own wellbeing and their staff." Building communication and trust in meetings and conversations enabled middle leaders to do more with the executive teams and to gradually develop the same level of agency and trust they had within their own departmental and pastoral teams. Building agency involves honesty:

> When you feel that you are trusted, when you feel that you are cared for, when you feel that yes, I can make mistakes because there's someone there to help you. There's no dictatorship that takes place here with the leaders: its collegial. It's working together. It's supporting each other and we know we make mistakes. We learn from them, we grow, we discuss.

Building trust takes time and authentic relationships, and these enable collegiality, risk-taking, and shared leadership. As one senior leader explained: "You can bring a cultural shift over time, but it takes a long time for people to trust you, that you mean what you say, that what you're doing is authentic, and that it's going to continue." The executive worked hard to build trust, and they knew it would take time to change the practices of leading together and change the image of middle leading in the school.

Fragmentation School: The Broken Mirror

Distorted mirrors can be reshaped over time. Mirrors can also be broken, and after they are shattered, they fail to reflect, leaving only the wooden back board. These mirrors can also be repaired, but the first step in repairing a broken mirror is realizing that it is broken in the first place. Fragmentation School (another metaphor) was embarking on a leadership project where middle leaders were expected to develop skills in work together more efficiently for student learning outcomes. In this school, the senior leadership team operated separately from the middle leadership team and wanted the hierarchical structure to remain tight. There were to be two levels of leading: middle leaders on the ground in classrooms, with students and staff, and senior leaders overseeing the work and advising solutions. Middle leaders were being given the opportunity to share their expertise and their issues with one another but had no influence over change or development with senior leadership. It was like a metaphor of a mirror with no glass – no reflection – only the back board. Leadership was not being mirrored between senior and middle leaders. As middle leaders were being constrained in their capacity to lead learning and wellbeing decisions, the level of mistrust grew. Senior executive made decisions without consultation, impacting agency. As one senior leader shared:

> Most of the senior school executive have pretty good relationships with the middle leaders. And most of them make the middle leaders feel safe and able to question. Occasionally some of them ride rough shot over people, or their ideas, but most of them are pretty good. Some senior leaders make decisions with minimal consultation or discussion, leaving

out people who could make valuable contributions to making excellent decisions and making changes really work well. They would be able to make much better decisions, changes, and create better opportunities for the student, and staff, if they were to consult more rather than making decisions hastily for the sake of saving time, to reach out and tread very carefully about who the stakeholders are.

Because communication was one-way, trust was not mirrored.

> When we meet, if someone is expressing an opinion which is contrary to that of the high-end senior leadership, then there is no psychological safety, and we watch our colleagues get shot down in flames for expressing opinions which are contrary... frank and fearless advice is not being treated as interaction, nor an opportunity for discussion and growth. Across teams there is not a sufficient opportunity to build capacity and share concerns. And so, decisions are made ad hoc, without consultation, and are not fully communicated without an opportunity to question them.

The hierarchy worked in a *power over* way rather than simply an *organising* and supporting way where people needed permission to do things. The middle leadership team is not being treated as a team or at least not on the same team as the executive. There is no consultation. They have permission to lead only in the middle, not beyond.

> It's one thing to have contribution to agenda, it's another thing to say none of you have sent me anything, so I'm cancelling the meeting. Some of the things that can come up when you meet, just don't come up so decisions get made without discussion.

Middle leaders may not have time to think of agenda items and won't share them if they think it is pointless. A lack of psychological safety is diminishing the capacity for communication to occur.

Listening skills are important, but without shared decision-making, there is no listening. The skills of speaking out and responding become brave, risky decisions that may be productive or damaging and may build or diminish trust.

> Trust that they can come and see you about something and have a robust conversation where you don't feel that you are going to be attacked, to be able to make a joint decision that is for the benefit of everyone. It's that modelling, that going to the source, don't just shoot it off and say why didn't you do this, or what happened? Model. Go and have the discussion.

People were able to identify the parts of the broken mirror and how it can be repaired: "Psychological safety and trust would allow that to happen. That combined with clear frequent honest communication and meetings. It always comes back to time, but it's also communication skills, the active listening, both giving."

The school changed the leadership structure so that middle leaders could work with many different leaders:

> The structure has changed with our senior leaders recently, enabling middle leaders to find more than one person to speak to. They can talk with our director of professional learning, or our head of wellbeing and bounce around ideas for deepening learning. They have people that they can tap into for support, for guidance, and growth, and take that back to their teams and empower teachers to effect change within their practice.

Changing structures didn't change the fragmentation but enabled a practical workaround, which was effective.

Cheval School: The Reflective Mirror

Everything in front of a mirror is reflected backwards. In this way, mirrors retrace backward paths as they reflect physical actions and practices. A cheval is a free standing mirror. Participants in Cheval School were able to trace back their path of change in leadership, enabling them to map their growth together over time and the trust that they developed together. *Relational trust* enabled the process.

> That's step 1. People were a bit unsure about the purpose of this work together at the beginning. I think that became quite clear in the first couple of sessions. The fact that we continued working with you, and it wasn't just, let's just *do* this workshop and then do what was always done. We made changes straight away. People being on board comes with relational trust. It was also overcoming some mindsets that were built on previous experiences. Open dialogues created an environment where people could bring their understandings and beliefs about the way things were done in a way that was non-confrontational. We were able to clear the air and get a better understanding of some of the barriers around a lack of trust in processes from the way things had been done previously.

The senior leadership team reflected in the mirror and knew that the best thing they could do was let go of decision-making:

> The relationship's meant to be built on trust, and that trust comes from the process. We were very mindful as the senior executive, about making sure that if we were going to open this dialogue and begin these

conversations, then we need to really be strong in supporting and being consistent with how we follow up. If we're going to ask for people to be involved, we need to just accept that even if it wasn't exactly the direction we wanted, we were going to put the trust in the work people are doing and accept what was going to happen as a result and really empower the team to make those decisions. Through those strong processes, that was the most powerful thing that we did ... People could see that regardless of what came up throughout the process, that we were going to support decisions that were being made and that we were going to follow through with what the team set out to achieve.

A positive working environment was not about having everything perfect but about having a process for progressing. Leading is not about a perfect reflection in the mirror but about having all colleagues engaged in looking:

For us it was about building relational trust amongst the executive team and having that positive climate where everyone would know that whatever it was that happened was being looked at or being developed so that everyone was on board and in it together. The improving phase – that's when you have a positive working environment.

The team reflected on the wider influences of education policy influencing their school, such as new role descriptions that increased workload for leaders because of the teacher shortage. They recognised that attributing blame to the leadership team was unproductive but that seeing the big picture might be helpful.

Trust in the senior executive and the system can be hard, because with new policies, it's not always there. Recognising it might not be a relationship you love but at the end of the day we are part of it.

Leaders focussed instead on the importance of what they could do and how they could contribute.

People are very keen to get involved, to have their say. No-one sits back. People feel that relational trust. Not everyone's always going to agree but it's important to have input and be part of the decision-making process. I think once you empower middle leaders, trust is a very fine line.

Solidarity was built from the changes in practices, a genuine care for each other, and a positive workplace with high psychological safety. As one senior leader shared: "We're so invested in the school; we call ourselves a family and love the school and students. The investment and connection, that's important. But between each other. Trust and relationship go together. Collective trust across the school is strong." Working relationships mirror trust.

Connecting Research and Practice

Relational trust is clearly important in schools, but how do we make a start on building trust if it doesn't exist or needs to be improved? One relatively simple way to start is by encouraging one aspect of relational trust which has been shown to have important effects on team effectiveness: psychological safety.

Psychological Safety

> If someone asked me what phrase I heard most often from my direct supervisor, I would immediately recall "Không em", which simply means "No" in English. This was his typical response whenever I proposed an idea or suggested a new way of doing something. Eventually, I stopped sharing what I truly thought and began waiting quietly for instructions instead.

Team psychological safety is "a shared belief held by members of a team that the team is safe for interpersonal risk taking" (Edmondson, 1999, p. 350). Teams with high psychological safety are teams where people can voice criticisms, suggestions, and ideas without fear of being rejected, embarrassed, or punished. Voice behaviour (speaking up) is normalized, and hard discussions can be had without fear. Psychological safety climate exists at three levels: the organization, the team, and dyads (relationships between two individuals). In our work with schools, we have found that psychological safety climate can be different at all three of these levels. For example, middle leaders may be able to speak up amongst themselves but not with the school executive. Or psychological safety may be strong in one department but not in another. Even within a team, relationships may differ between pairs in the group. We are all familiar with this difference in our relationships – we can be more comfortable voicing our opinions with one person than perhaps with another.

This climate of lowered interpersonal risk has been extensively researched at the team level and is linked to both wellbeing and team performance (Edmondson & Bransby, 2023). It is important when there is change, uncertainty, and interdependence between individuals, such as when collaboration is required. We argue that these are the conditions that educators face in schools, and this is backed by research (Edmondson et al., 2016).

Psychological safety research and theory allow us to use educator silence (as seen in the quote above) or voice as one indicator of trust. We can then start to listen carefully to understand what is driving silence. For example, educators may not speak up due to fear (this is known as quiescent silence) or due to learned hopelessness based on experiences of nothing changing (known as acquiescent silence) (Kassandrinou et al., 2023). Team psychological safety varies depending on context and may also be more complex in countries with high levels of power distance (Hu et al., 2018), as described by the middle leader in the following quote:

Like me, many Vietnamese teachers tend to prefer clear direction rather than open-ended discussions, which often feel vague and inappropriate in a hierarchical context. I have recognised in both myself and many of my Vietnamese staff a strong orientation toward power distance. What makes things even more complex is that there is individual variation in how teachers interpret and respond to power distance, even within the same cultural setting. This contrast is especially noticeable at my international school in southern Vietnam, where local and expatriate teachers work together. One clear example is the silence from Vietnamese staff during meetings, especially when engaging with foreign colleagues or school leaders. It is not a sign of disengagement or lack of ideas but rather a culturally shaped response rooted in concerns about contradicting others in public or feeling uncertain about using a second language.

Benefits of Psychological Safety

A major review paper of 185 research studies in 2023 identified four key themes in the research on psychological safety relevant to this book: "getting things done, learning behaviours, improving the work experience, and leadership" (Edmondson & Bransby, 2023).

Getting Things Done

A key theme in the psychological safety literature is enabling performance. The literature provides compelling evidence that psychological safety enhances team performance by enabling clear communication and coordination of activities (Edmondson & Bransby, 2023). Psychological safety may enable teaching teams to get things done by removing barriers to both individual and team performance and allowing schools to adapt to changing circumstances.

There are clear examples of psychological safety enabling communication in the discussion of Cheval School, for example: "people are very keen to get involved, to have their say". In Cheval School, the team worked hard to improve the already strong relational trust in the school, including the uncomfortable work of identifying and addressing misconceptions about the operation of the executive team. This demonstrated to us that even relatively small changes in this area can lead to positive outcomes. In other cases, psychological safety can vary at different levels; for example, in Fragmentation School, a member of the leadership team worked hard to listen to teachers in the school and to pass this information on anonymously, even though people did not feel safe to raise it directly with the executive team.

Learning Behaviours

Psychological safety plays an important role in learning and knowledge-sharing as well as creativity and innovation (Edmondson & Bransby, 2023).

The interaction between psychological safety and performance standards can be understood using a 2-by-2 matrix (Edmondson, 2018). The best outcomes occur in the "learning and high-performance zone", where there is high psychological safety and high-performance standards. This zone allows people to learn from each other and to work together effectively on complex problems.

Improving the Work Experience

Psychological safety can improve the experience of work by allowing people to be themselves and by fostering an inclusive climate (Edmondson & Bransby, 2023). The quote from a middle leader below illustrates both the complexity and potential benefits of building psychological safety.

> In a culturally diverse workplace like mine, where people have different communication styles and cultural expectations, it raises a real question: does psychological safety truly exist for everyone? That said, developing psychological safety in a Vietnamese international school involves more than simply encouraging people to speak up. It means understanding the different expectations and creating structures and relationships where everyone feels respected, safe to contribute, and most importantly genuinely heard.
>
> In my context, fostering psychological safety requires school leaders and those in middle leadership roles like mine to adopt a culturally proficient approach. Leaders need to learn how to create spaces that invite open dialogue. Foreign teachers need to learn how to navigate local cultural norms, while local teachers and staff need to build confidence in sharing their ideas. This means creating genuine moments of connection where both the speaker and the listener are fully present and engaged in the conversation. This is especially important in my diverse context, where Vietnamese and foreign teachers, as well as school leaders, bring different cultural expectations.

Leadership

The research shows that three key practices are critical: to build psychological safety leaders need to listen, show competence in their role, and be transparent. The importance and challenges of listening are illustrated clearly in this quote from a Vietnamese middle leader:

> For all of us, it means learning to listen not to reject ideas because they are different from ours, but to understand the thinking behind them. For example, instead of saying "No" to a suggestion, we can ask the following to invite responses "What are the benefits of your approach?" or "Can you explain why the other option might not work?". In the end, psychological safety for me is not about having no fear, but listening carefully and responding kindly, even when it's hard to do so.

Trust in Schools

Trust can be an intangible term. It is important to clarify exactly what we mean by educative trust. Can teachers trust each other in a climate of performativity and still seek the best for their students? Can leaders trust others in moments where accountability policies seem to suggest that the system does not trust them? Trust between educators is about regard for the other: encouraging their capacity to deliver, to speak honestly, to be true to their word, and to act consistently. Trust makes generous assumptions about the intentions of others and verifies these through action. Trust is ultimately about respect.

Trust builds working relationships. Research in English schools has shown that trust between teachers and leaders has a positive impact on school improvement (Day et al., 2016). Transparency, measurement, accountability, and competition have created the need for verification, which has the potential to build mistrust in schools. Accountability is increasing suspicion (Fink & McCulla, 2016). Educative trust balances accountability and excellence in teaching and learning alongside valuing all humans and seeking their belonging and membership in the school. In considering the psychosocial wellbeing of staff, we are not suggesting that we are creating a wellbeing/performance dichotomy where performance does not matter. Wellbeing is linked with team performance.

There are many kinds of trust. Relational trust is built in schools through interpersonal trust where there is mutual professional respect, interactional trust with safe dialogue, intersubjective trust where modelling occurs alongside collegiality, intellectual trust where people have confidence in each other's capabilities, and pragmatic trust where realistic goals and expectations are established (Edwards-Groves et al., 2016). These are all built through the practices of encouraging voice, reflection, and sharing.

Pedagogical trust is about respect for the decisions and actions of educators. It may look like letting people experiment with a new idea or being non-judgmental toward a colleague, as the scenarios above suggest. It might mean being open-minded about different philosophies of education where classrooms do not all look the same. A teacher who is given pedagogical trust understands the boundaries and choice in which they can teach, and they know they are seen as a reliable educator who can teach well, action change, and lead learning. They are free to be innovative and accountable for student progress; they listen and share whilst keeping confidentiality; they are driven by student needs whilst upholding the values of the school and are non-judgmental whilst being willing to take risks to learn and evaluate learning. In a climate of trust, leaders trust teachers and teachers trust leaders. Trust is choosing to risk making something you value vulnerable to another person's actions (Grice, 2018).

Trust is built in the smallest educative moments in schools. The practices of trust include listening, responding, and acting upon those responses where words and actions are aligned. Trust admits mistakes. Trust takes on feedback and works on it. Communication is open, honest, and sincere. It verifies and asks for ways to improve. Trust builds up others, celebrating their successes publicly and privately. Trust thanks people. It cares for the other. Trust puts your ego aside, which is why leadership hierarchies require care in building trust. Trust is demonstrated in consistent action. It builds clarity and accountability. Repeated acts of integrity are needed to nurture trust (Day, 2013). Trust is brave. It has boundaries that are created together. It is non-judgmental and generous (Brown, 2015).

The practices of trust build psychological safety. Psychological safety refers specifically to whether people can use their voice in the school environment to ask questions, raise issues, make suggestions, and admit mistakes. Psychological safety is foundational to wellbeing and performance in dynamic environments where there is a commitment to excellence. It comes through open dialogue, humility, and putting other people first. Some of the practices of leadership and leadership progression in schools go against a culture of psychological safety, which is a shame.

Pedagogical trust is enabled by leading change together. The lesser alternative is compliance (Grice, 2018). Trust is not compliance (Browning, 2013; O'Neill, 2002). An example of a workplace that discovered that professional productivity increased when members of a team most needed to feel they could speak up and share ideas, challenges, and concerns without fear of embarrassment or humiliation is Project Aristotle at Google, which challenged conventional understandings of how effective teams function.

Democratic engagement that builds trust is integral to the project of education that builds society (Freire, 1985). Respect transforms trust (Edwards-Groves et al., 2016). Trust is reciprocal and is more valued by teachers than it is by leaders in schools (Fink & McCulla, 2016).

Principals trusted teachers whom they saw as ethical and who acted morally by putting students first (Fink, 2016). A Canadian school principal stated: "those I trust more, I do not verify their work as often. I ask for less proof of data and evidence of student learning" (Fink, 2016, p. 87). The opposite of trust is the infantilisation of adults. We are all familiar with the image of the powerful principal who disciplines students, where orderly control is seen as safe, virtuous, and professional. When adults discipline other adults as if they are children still coming to maturity, these is known as infantilization (Kant, 2007; Keij, 2021). Infantilisation is inappropriately disciplining a colleague as if they were a child (Guattari, 2009; Kant, 2007; Postman, 1982, Stiegler, 2010) and is under-researched in educational leadership research (Grice, 2025).

Fitzgerald (2009) suggests that the continuing lack of trust in teachers has resulted in a climate of performance management in education where the mistrust of teachers has resulted in "teacher-proofed schools that deny the professionalism of teachers" (p. 45). A climate of mistrust fosters a compliance culture that minimises professionalism (O'Neill, 2002). This looks like treating adults like children and telling them what to do, not allowing them space to think and act and make their own choices.

Collaboration is unsustainable without trust (Mishra, 1996). Working together is not enough. Shared understanding matters (Grice et al., 2023). Leaders can choose practices that build trust such as through considered communication, embracing rather than avoiding problems and issues, valuing social gatherings and interactions with colleagues, and using humour and shared decision-making.

Renewal for Strategic Direction: The Problem with Change Champions

Change champions are people on a team who will take the initiative (Kotter, 2008). During times of change, change champions can support the strategic direction of a school; however, it may not build a whole school culture of change as resisters will continue to refuse to change. Renewal is the hard work of leadership, which means supporting the people you have rather than a revolving door of new staff. Renewal can happen by creating cultures of trust and psychological safety where whole school teams work together in the project of change with every person through pairs, teams, and whole staff. Renewal begins by making generous assumptions about people whilst giving them the space to be honest about their capacity.

When it comes to strategic change and syllabus reform, we need to see the project and the people in realistic ways. People are the project of education. When difficulties arise, rather than skipping difficult conversations, ask people how they can be supported, and if you notice that that they may be struggling, create an environment where they can speak up. Create a culture where though collaborative job crafting, they may be able to move to a role that better suits their strengths. The job of a leader is to understand people's strengths. Taking a stance of wonder rather than having limited views or self-fulfilling prophecies of how teams can work supports team communication. Curiosity and listening may give people the stability they need to stay, by building psychological safety. Change avoiders sometimes lack confidence and may need support to develop skills as well.

Sometimes school leaders utilise the idea of "change champions" to build their own psychological safety, such as having a trusted deputy or executive team. These close relationships are important, but it is helpful for executive leaders to be mindful of when these relationships are impacting the psychological safety of the larger team because this is where change champions fall – where there are change champions and passive resisters on the bench, change hasn't taken place at all. In these environments, change champions run the risk of burnout and risk their own psychological safety as people resist them further dividing the staff.

Relational trust is built by participants from the view that leaders hold of them before they even speak. Leaders need to hold the person before them and the direction they are keen to head with both hands so that trust can be built. When a project or strategy makes people seem invisible, people become the problem. People without strategy is stasis. Putting people before strategy is required.

Communicative Learning Spaces

Communication practices became integral to the changes the leaders at Eager School introduced. When voice is enabled, speaking and listening become part of a team's shared identity. Communicative learning spaces (Sjølie et al., 2018; Goldshaft & Sjølie, 2024) are democratic, safe, and supportive communication spaces that invite other people's voices.

Power hierarchies deter communicative learning spaces, and this calls for different leadership practices (Goldshaft & Sjølie, 2024), beyond instructing, to be collaborative. Where learning and sharing are not hierarchical, communication strategies are required to navigate the unspoken politics of rules and power, to hear equal voice, and to build consensus. As communicative learning spaces develop, practices, including listening, understanding, building solidarity, and learning, are integral to these learning spaces and communicative interactions.

Gaines' (2007) communicative theory of leadership practice connects communication and practices by identifying eight core practices of leadership: (1) reporting and inquiring, (2) building dialogue and facilitating, (3) directing and pledging, (4) building commitment and obligation, (5) envisioning and advocating, (6) inspiring and motivating, (7) declaring, constituting, and creating, and (8) changing social reality. Each of these practices forms part of how teachers and leaders can work together, and they align with our ideas on leading. Our work is distinct in that it invites people to work together collectively.

Leading in Practice

While the research on interventions to increase psychological safety is still developing, there are recommended practices that leaders can apply to increase voices in their team and build the shared belief that it is safe to speak up (Edmondson, 2018). These practices include the following:

1 **Setting the stage** involves clear communication of the situation and why input is needed. Careful use of language can help in shifting assumptions about the cause of failures and errors from individual incompetence to understanding the complexity of the situation. For example, let's imagine Min (assistant principal) meeting with Sami (year 8 coordinator) and Chris (science teacher) about Quinn, a student in Chris's

class. Quinn had become upset in the science class yesterday, yelled at Chris, and run out of the room and then out the school gate. Min might set the stage by saying "Thank you for meeting with me. I am very concerned about Quinn after the incident yesterday and need your input to try and understand what is happening and what we should do next to ensure her safety."

2 **Inviting participation** involves situational humility by leaders. In this step, leaders emphasize that they don't have all the answers in this situation and want to draw on the combined expertise of everyone in the team to work out a way forward. For example, Min might invite participation by saying, "You both know Quinn better than I do, so I don't have all the answers here. I want to hear your thoughts on this so we can develop a plan. Chris, could you tell us your perspective on what happened, and anything else you might know that's relevant?" We're very aware that this may not be how leaders usually communicate in schools, but demonstrating humility in complex situations is an important part of creating an educational setting that decreases interpersonal risk and utilizes the expertise of all educators.

3 **Responding productively** involves respectful communication that helps people to understand that their input is valued. This increases the chances that they will speak up in the future. Being careful with words, tone, and body language can help prevent people from feeling embarrassed, dismissed, or punished. For example, let's imagine Chris is frustrated and immediately suggests that Quinn should be moved to a different class. If Min responds productively, there is a greater chance that the discussion can continue and help everyone to build a better understanding of Quinn. Min could say something like "I can hear how frustrated you are, and that's certainly an option. But before we decide, could you tell me more about what happened and why you think changing class might be the best option?"

It's easy to imagine here that there is a history to the interactions between Chris and Quinn and that Chris has not felt comfortable seeking help with the situation. If this meeting goes well, Chris may in the future feel more able to speak up before the situation escalates. By using these leadership practices, Min can help to create psychological safety in the school and increase the opportunity for problems to be addressed before they escalate as well as benefiting from the knowledge of everyone involved.

Practice Menu

Working relationships are built by trust which in turn builds psychological safety. Trust is built by making generous assumptions of others, verifying, listening and communicating, reflecting, and building solidarity through shared decision-making in teams. Clear meeting protocols that encourage voice and active listening can support relationship-building.

Current practices	Questions about practice arrangements	Suggested practices for application
Sayings (communication) How do I show that I listen to others? How do I share my views? Do I/we say yes or no here? Do I say sorry? Do I say thank you?	*Cultural-discursive arrangements* Do I praise others? What meeting protocols do we have that ensure everyone is heard? Are there mandates in our school – or consultations?	1 Mirror task: reflect on the leadership imaginary in your school. How do people see leadership in your school? 2 What is the level of trust in your school? Complete the survey on job satisfaction. 3 Make generous assumptions of others whilst verifying. Be non-judgmental.
Doings Am I using meeting protocols and active listening? Do I trust myself to do a good job? Am I reliable, consistent, and equitable?	*Material-economic arrangements* Do I support others? Do we work together?	4 Set the stage for speaking and listening by modelling active listening and careful speaking. Develop communication practices that support psychological safety.
Relatings Am I leading and modelling trust by making generous assumptions of others whilst verifying? Am I aware of cultural differences between people in my team?	*Social-political arrangements* Can I trust others to do their job? Do I have generous assumptions of others? Do I recognise strengths in others?	5 Rather than change champions, work with and value everyone to build solidarity. Expect passive resisters and listen to their concerns.
Dispositions (habitus) Do I respect others? How bossy am I? How safe is our school to work in as a teacher? Do I recognise my weaknesses and acknowledge them?	*Practice traditions* Are we bringing out the best in all our leaders and teachers? Can people be themselves? Does our workplace welcome diversity and include everyone? How do we cope with stress?	6 Invite participation using protocols such as Circle of Voices and clear meeting protocols. 7 Respond productively to feedback. Check in on your zone.

Summary of Key Points

- Trust matters in schools for staff and student wellbeing, student attainment, and school improvement.
- Trust is built in the smallest educative moments in schools.
- Trust is mirrored in perception and action.
- Pedagogical trust involves agency, choice, and consensus.
- Trust involves making generous assumptions about the intentions of others and verifying these through action.

- A climate of trust is where leaders trust teachers and teachers trust leaders.
- Listening and to speaking are habits of psychological safety.
- Meeting protocols support trust and psychological safety.

References

Brown, B. (2015). *Daring Greatly: How the Courage to Be Vulnerable Transforms the Way We Live, Love, Parent, and Lead.* New York: Avery.

Browning, P. (2013). Creating the conditions for transformational change. *Australian Educational Leader,* 35(3), 14–17.

Day, C. (2013). How to trust others to take the lead. *School Leadership Today* 4(6), 68–76.

Day, C., Gu, Q., & Sammons, P. (2016). The impact of leadership on student outcomes: How successful school leaders use transformational and instructional strategies to make a difference. *Educational Administration Quarterly,* 52(2), 221–258. DOI:10.1177/0013161X15616863

Edmondson, A. (1999). Psychological safety and learning behavior in work teams. *Administrative Science Quarterly,* 44(2), 350–383.

Edmondson, A. (2018). *The Fearless Organization: Creating Psychological Safety in the Workplace for Learning, Innovation, and Growth.* Hoboken, NJ: John Wiley & Sons.

Edmondson, A.C., & Bransby, D.P. (2023). Psychological safety comes of age: Observed themes in an established literature. *Annual Review of Organizational Psychology and Organizational Behavior,* 10(1), 55–78.

Edmondson, A.C., Higgins, M., Singer, S., & Weiner, J. (2016). Understanding psychological safety in health care and education organizations: A comparative perspective. *Research in Human Development,* 13(1), 65–83.

Edwards-Groves, C., Grootenboer, P., & Ronnerman, K. (2016). Facilitating a culture of relational trust in school-based action research: Recognising the role of middle leaders, *Educational Action Research,* 24(3), 369–386, DOI:10.1080/09650792.2015.1131175

Fink, D. (2016). Trust and mistrust: Competing models of policy and practice. In *Trust and Verify: The Real Keys to School Improvement. An international Examination of Trust and Distrust in Seven Countries.* UCL: IOE Press.

Fink, D., & McCulla, N. (2016). Trust and verify. In *Trust and Verify: The Real Keys to School Improvement. An International Examination of Trust and Distrust in Seven Countries.* London: UCL, IOE Press: University College London.

Fitzgerald, T. (2009). The tyranny of bureaucracy. *Educational Management, Leadership and Administration,* 37(1), 51–65.

Freire, P. (1970). *Pedagogy of the Oppressed.* New York: Seabury.

Freire, P. (1985). *The Politics of Education: Culture, Power and Liberation.* London: Bergin and Garvey.

Gaines, K.A. (2007). *A communicative theory of leadership practice.* Doctoral dissertation, Antioch University. http://rave.ohiolink.edu/etdc/view?acc_num=antioch1193149740

Goldshaft, B., & Sjølie, E. (2024). Creating communicative learning spaces in initial teacher education (ITE) with observation-grounded co-mentoring practices, *Professional Development in Education,* 50(3), 533–550. DOI:10.1080/19415257.2024.2337772

Grice, C. (2018). Leading pedagogical reform. *International Journal of Leadership in Education, 22*(3), 355–370. DOI:10.1080/13603124.2018.1463462

Grice, C. (2025), *The Practices of Leading Pedagogy*. Singapore: Springer.

Grice, C., Seiser, A.F., & Wilkinson, J. (2023). Decentring pedagogical leadership: Educational leading as a pedagogical practice. *Journal of Educational Administration and History, 55*(1), 89–107. DOI:10.1080/00220620.2022.2163381

Guattari, F. (2009). So what. In S. Lotringer (Ed.), *Soft Subversions* (pp. 64–80). Los Angeles: Semiotext(e).

Hu, J., Erdogan, B., Jiang, K., Bauer, T.N., & Liu, S. (2018). Leader humility and team creativity: The role of team information sharing, psychological safety, and power distance. *Journal of Applied Psychology, 103*(3), 313.

Kant, I. (2007). Lectures on pedagogy. In G. Zöller & R. B. Louden (Eds.), *Anthropology, History, and Education* (pp. 434–485). Cambridge, UK: Cambridge University Press.

Kassandrinou, M., Lainidi, O., Mouratidis, C., & Montgomery, A. (2023). Employee silence, job burnout and job engagement among teachers: The mediational role of psychological safety. *Health Psychology and Behavioral Medicine, 11*(1). DOI:10.1080/21642850.2023.2213302

Keij, D. (2021). Immature adults and playing children: On Bernard Stiegler's critique of infantilization. *Studies in Philosophy of Education, 40*, 67–80. DOI:10.1007/s11217-020-09742-9

Kotter, J.P. (2008). *Force for Change: How Leadership Differs from Management*. New York: Simon and Schuster.

Mishra, A.K. (1996). Organisational response to crisis: The centrality of trust. In R. Kramer & T. Tyler (Eds.), *Trust in Organisations: Frontiers of Theory and Research* (pp. 261–287). Thousand Oaks, CA: Sage.

O'Neill, O. (2002). *A Question of Trust: The BBC Reith Lectures*. Cambridge, UK: Cambridge.

Postman, N. (1982). *The Disappearance of Childhood*. New York: Delacorte.

Sjølie, E., Francisco, S., & Langelotz, L. (2018). Communicative learning spaces and learning to become a teacher. *Pedagogy, Culture & Society, 27*(3), 365–382. DOI:10.1080/14681366.2018.1500392

Stiegler, B. (2010). Taking care of youth and the generations. *Meridian: Crossing Aesthetics*. Redwood City, CA: Stanford University Press.

5 The Expansive Role of Leaders
What do You do, What Could We do?

How often do we really ask '*What do we need?*' as school leaders? More specifically, *What do we need to do to work together better, to get everything done, and to not burn out in the process?* Asking is the first step in identifying problems and the practices that need to change the way we lead. This chapter invites you to think about how to gain more sustainable workloads across your school. The chapter outlines a step-by-step process for balancing job demands and resources to individually craft their role in line with their purpose and practices. The individual job crafting process, a way of designing your role, we are suggesting is aligned with action research, which formed the basis for the theory of practice architectures. We also need to recover from work. This chapter also encapsulates the necessary practices for work recovery, which are after work actions that support your recovery from work.

> Do what you can with what you have where you are.
> - Theodore Roosevelt n.d., attributed to Squire Bill Widener

Examples from Schools

For the past two decades, educational leadership research has shown that leadership is distributed. For some, this means delegated; for others, dumped. However, Woods and Roberts (2019) have shown that leadership is distributed through people's decisions and actions. This happens regardless of whether leaders decide that it should be, nor because tasks are shared, or responsibility is devolved or dumped among others, nor through leaders interactions. People choose to accept or reject leadership decisions and lead themselves accordingly. In this chapter, school leaders are invited to reflect on their changing roles, how they lead pedagogy, and how they could lead together to improve learning and wellbeing.

If we think about leading as a process rather than an outcome, static job descriptions may not encapsulate everything we do and how schools are changing.

Other industries have recognised that static role descriptions do not fit their rapidly changing work environments and are adopting a more dynamic set of team models and approaches. Adopting innovative ways of thinking about leading enables us to negotiate and change tasks and practices with colleagues, sharing loads and choosing to take on and to leave behind practices in accordance with our values and purpose.

Middle leaders are central to the pedagogy and wellbeing of a school. They typically see themselves as other people see them, existing as part of a hierarchy within a school where they are the midpoint between teachers and senior leaders:

> Alongside my director, I work with six homeroom teachers who are the primary touchstone for the wellbeing needs of students in our house. Our school utilises a typical bureaucratic structure meaning I am the midway point between the senior leadership team and the homeroom teachers. The middle leader role is a central role, a difficult role sometimes being in the middle, even though most schools are trying not to see it in that hierarchical way, it is a hierarchical position. And sometimes, as the name suggests, they are caught in the middle.

This chapter invites a different view. Middle leaders need support from senior leaders to navigate difficult wellbeing situations and curriculum mandates and effect whole school change in pedagogy and wellbeing, but rather than a situation where their position limits their capacity to lead pedagogy and wellbeing, what is needed a shift from *me*, to *we*, to *us*.

If teams of leaders in schools were to wonder not only *What do you do?* but *Who are we?* and *What could we do?*, the possibilities for schools to know students and how they learn would be greatly enhanced. Sadly, so many schools are stuck in thinking about role descriptions: *What do you do?* instead of *What makes us leaders of pedagogy, learning and wellbeing together?* Middle leaders lead pedagogy, learning, and wellbeing most beneficially and effectively when they work together with other middle leaders. Middle leaders function together best when the middle leadership team works effectively with the senior leadership team. Sadly, research and experience show that this is rare. People can work cohesively on a shared priority through job crafting and work design. It is far easier than people think and yet it seems to be a seismic shift in practice for school leadership teams.

It is standard practice to commence a position with a role description that guides the expected tasks and competencies required to lead. Role descriptions need to be comprehensive and accurate because this provides role clarity to everyone. People who lead with initiative work beyond their role descriptions or tailor the role to their talents. School leaders craft their jobs every day. People tend to start their day in school with the required tasks: teaching lessons and attending meetings. They then tend to decide when and how they will do other tasks such as planning, assessing, marking, and resourcing their teaching, meeting with others, and engaging with parents and students. These decisions depend upon a whole range of factors, including their energy levels, their engagement with their team, their enthusiasm for the task, and their personal lives. Time management is also a factor. These are things we all know and do but don't think about too much. We argue that people work in accordance with their strengths, and one of their strengths may be selecting challenging tasks, depending on their level of confidence and the level of psychological safety in the school. We teach people how to craft their jobs in accordance with a key priority.

At Vinaya School (a pseudonym that means *to lead*, in Sanskrit), highly competent middle leaders were crafting their jobs and were able to talk about it. They used sticky notes to write down what they valued doing together to determine their key priority. These middle leaders were valued for their strengths and their adaptability:

> I see the middle leader doing a lot of the core business of the school. At our school, either leading in wellbeing or leading in learning. Playing out operationally, the strategic vision and leading teams. It's important that they're not micromanaged so that they're able to use their own strengths to lead their teams. It's the middle of everything. You seek advice and management from those above you, but you also lead within your team and depending on how you view yourself within the school, different projects or different areas.

Middle leaders are supported with individual job crafting skills to support the limited time they have and their levels of stress and for their wellbeing.

> The barriers that I hear from the middle leaders are time. Continuing attention to admin requirements takes them away from making time to collaborate across departments.

Middle leaders are also highly skilled and capable professionals who seem to lack agency in some schools. Individual job crafting equips them to be creative and in control of their work as well as equipping others in their team to lead initiatives: "I support middle leaders to develop strong teaching teams that can take some of that weight of responsibility or administration and give our teachers more opportunities for leadership which would give middle leaders back some time."

Connecting Research and Practice

A middle leader made changes to work design in an attempt to reduce burnout in a school in Vietnam and explained what they gained from learning together in community:

> I've found that in practice, it's not easy to directly reduce demands. When parents or students send an email, both parents and supervisors

expect immediate responses and often within the same day! In my experience, instead of just "reduce demands", combining small adjustments with meaningful opportunities for professional growth has had a more realistic effect on motivation and engagement. For example, I observed that some experienced teachers were becoming disengaged, as their routines began to contribute to feelings of burnout. In response, I invited them to lead professional learning communities, allowing them to be "challenged" in new, purposeful ways. At the same time, this also supported new teachers by helping to close the gap between them and their more experienced colleagues, a gap often reinforced by the significant power distance within the school culture. In my context, interactions between established and new staff were limited to formal meetings focused on information delivery rather than meaningful collaboration or knowledge sharing.

Leading and Learning with Others

Schools have leaders in a range of positions because the task of leading pedagogy and wellbeing requires teams of people to take on the tasks of curriculum reform, pastoral care, and teaching well. Principals and senior leaders are typically not in classrooms full time leading learning and instead lead whole-scale projects. Middle leaders are also given a teaching load and time to lead initiatives in schools as well. In this way, it could be argued that leadership is distributed (Spillane, 2006).

Distributed leadership (Spillane, 2006) is a theory that espouses sharing leadership among others. How people see leadership as being shared varies from thinking that simply performing different roles is sharing, to navigating tasks between people as new situations arise. Woods and Roberts (2015) argue that regardless of whether you think you are leading an initiative and people are following or not, distributed leadership is a fact. That is, people make active decisions to agree with a decision and follow through with it, to ignore it, or do the opposite all the time. In this way, despite any mandate, they believe that people lead themselves, particularly in schools and classrooms behind closed doors where they have the capacity and control to choose the extent to which they are going to enact any initiative and how. Consensus is the most powerful way forward. Some academics refer to this as 'genuinely distributed leadership', where accountability is shared and teaching and learning outcomes are positively affected (Gurr et al., 2005; Lakomski & Evers, 2017), as opposed to contrived forms of distribution, known as delegating or dumping, where one person sets a vision and the others simply follow or refuse. Asking other leaders to perform a task is not distributing leadership, and interactions (Leithwood et al., 2020) are also inadequate ways of understanding how to lead together. Distribution is about decision-making. The extent to which distributed leadership brings trust depends on the extent to which people collaborate or compete and the extent to which they learn together, like the school in Vietnam.

Distributed leadership is a process approach to leadership about the actions or practices of multiple leaders, ideally taking the focus off a single, heroic leader. As learning is by nature non-hierarchical, leading teams of educators as learners means distributing understanding, ideas, and initiatives amongst those closest and furthest from the action. Wenger (1998) sees this form of learning as a professional learning community.

Understanding how leading may be distributed amongst a team of school leaders may sound obvious and yet, as Hall (2013) critically analysed, it can be misunderstood. The agency of distributed leadership seems like a contradiction in hierarchies (Grice, 2018) or a misfit (Harris, 2014). School structures may limit or enable the capacity of middle leaders to lead pedagogy. Principals are responsible for distributing leadership for agency and autonomy (Day & Armstrong, 2016; Gronn, 2017), and this means letting others lead initiatives and involving teams in vision and strategy to grow initiatives, sustain teams, and reduce burnout.

On the surface, distributed leadership amongst middle leaders can appear democratic, but only certain people are authorised to influence goals and initiatives (Youngs, 2017). There is a clear distinction between distribution and autonomy and that is dependent upon trust. As middle leaders take on more responsibility and more leadership is distributed their way, middle leaders straddle 'playing the game' as team captain, to maintain the respect of their team, whilst also being asked to coach their team (Grootenboer, 2018). This metaphor brings insight into the autonomous opportunities that team captains have in middle leadership as game players and that coaches may lack on the sidelines. Middle leaders translate, interpret, and implement curriculum and policy. The responsibility is already theirs. Teams of leaders in schools decide how they play the game. This middle leader in the learning community in the school in Vietnam also understood the difference between sharing and distributing leadership and what it meant for learning together:

> While many new teachers at my school need the clarity, structure, and practical insights that effective knowledge sharing provides, this is nearly impossible perhaps due to the sense of hierarchy and the belief that expertise belongs solely to those with more experience and cannot be "shared". This made me wonder if experienced teachers and staff often felt stress and burnout because they didn't want to share, leaving them to carry it alone? In this sense, I truly believe that encouraging and learning to share knowledge to newer members of the school is a practical way to [build] a more connected and collaborative culture at my workplace. To complement the PLCs [professional learning communities], monthly Learning Circles were also introduced. These were informal yet structured sessions where teachers could share classroom practices, reflect on challenges, and exchange ideas or stories in a relaxed space. These gatherings fostered open yet respectful dialogue and offered a psychologically safe environment where all voices could be heard. Together, the PLCs and Learning

Circles created space for both professional growth and personal connection, easing the gap often experienced by newer staff at my workplace and re-engaging more experienced teachers with a renewed sense of purpose.

Distributed leadership is what you can do to facilitate job crafting in practice, by how things are shared out. In this way distributing leadership connects with job crafting.

The Practices of Leading

The theory of practice architectures suggests that leading is a co-experienced, interactive, dialogic, and intersubjective practice (English & Ehrich, 2017). Leading (the verb rather than the noun, leadership, as Wilkinson and Kemmis, 2014 write) is critical in order to understand what to do rather than just who you are. Wilkinson (2017) sees leading as a critical and socially just practice that enables participants and leading practices to be transformed so that praxis, or action that comes from your values, might be realised. The theory of practice architectures (Kemmis et al., 2014; Wilkinson, 2017, 2021) suggests that leading is a practice that happens in the intersubjective spaces between people including leaders, teachers, and students (Wilkinson, 2021; Grice, 2018; Edwards-Groves et al., 2022). A practice approach looks beyond the assumptions of leadership titles, recognising that leading practices influence other practices. As leading practices, such as administrating, communicating, and strategising, happen between people within social sites of schooling, it is recognised that leading is not necessarily carried out by one person but is reciprocal. This is known as the practice turn of educational leadership (Wilkinson, 2021) which emphasises the practices of leading over leadership roles. Wilkinson (2021) argues that pedagogical practices are practices of educational leading. We have argued together that understanding leading as a pedagogical practice is important for educators and students (Grice et al., 2023) and further that when our conceptual focus is on the practices of leading, practices make sense (Grice et al., 2023). Given that pedagogy means to *lead the child*, leading is part of pedagogy (Grice, 2025).

Leading Pedagogy

Teachers lead wellbeing and pedagogy. The IDEAS (Innovative Designs for Enhancing Achievements in Schools) professional learning model, highlighted teacher leadership as essential for pedagogical change and improved student learning outcomes (Andrews et al., 2004; Chew & Andrews, 2010). Teacher leadership is a form of autonomous distributed leadership. The alternative is 'control' decision-making (Blase & Blase, 1998). Perhaps the disconnect we see in schools between leading and pedagogy is about much more than power and autonomy. An increase in disillusion with the profession from teachers themselves is a direct result of an underemphasis on pedagogy. Diminishing pedagogy lies at the heart of the wrong turn we have taken in education, away from leading the child and towards instructing or instruction of students (and teachers), which leads to inequitable, contestable, and problematic outcomes. This calls for a return to an understanding not of curriculum, nor instruction, but of pedagogy, by whom, with whom, and for whom and for what purpose (Grice, 2025).

Leading in Practice

There are numerous ways we can make our work more sustainable by focusing on those aspects of work that are under our control. Two lines of research that are potentially helpful focus on recovery from work and job crafting as a means of adaptive self-regulation when work demands are high and resources are insufficient (Bakker & De Vries, 2021). Leaders can help by supporting and encouraging these strategies.

Recovery from Work

Active efforts to recover from work demands are a form of proactive work behaviour that can help us to work sustainably. This requires us to identify the effects of work demands (e.g., rumination, stress or anxiety, and fatigue) and match these with recovery experiences that help, in our experience, to address them (Sonnentag et al., 2022). For example, if you experience negative work-related rumination, then activities that help you to psychologically detach may be helpful (Sonnentag et al., 2022).

> I still remember a few years ago, when I was interviewed for my current role as a Coordinator at my international school in Vietnam. One of the questions asked was whether I would be willing to work on Saturdays, even though the official working hours were Monday to Friday. Being willing to work beyond the official working hours is seen as a sign of motivation and commitment, almost like an unofficial requirement for getting the job.
>
> At my school, work often spills over into home time, not just for line managers like me but also for teachers. Grading, planning, communicating with parents, and so much more, they rarely fit neatly into the school day. With the never-ending workload, it has become almost normal to feel obligated to work overtime and on weekends. Over time, it becomes harder to see the difference between work time and personal time, making it harder to fully detach.

This educator clearly describes the impact of relentless work demands that intrude into their personal life. Research shows that the ability to stop thinking about work, known as psychological detachment, is an important aspect of work-related recovery (Sonnentag et al., 2022). This may be particularly important when our thoughts about work are repetitive and negative (known as rumination) rather than positive or solution-focused (Tuerktorun et al.,

2020). So, if we are thinking about something positive from our day (e.g., a nice interaction with a student), that can be helpful for our wellbeing, but if we are ruminating over a negative event without a clear path forward, this is more likely to result in negative emotions, as illustrated below:

> There have been times when I felt so stressed and burnt out that I kept thinking about work until I was completely exhausted and passed out from tiredness. The next day, I would notice the same signs in my team, with low energy and low engagement after the long hours they had pushed through the day before.

Research backs up this educator's experience: spending periods of time each day where we are not thinking about work helps to reduce negative emotions. Research on educators in particular suggests that work stress and overload may reduce psychological detachment by increasing negative emotions and hence increasing rumination (Tuerktorun et al., 2020).

Support for recovery from leaders is critical, as the same educator describes:

> I still remember my supervisor once telling me "Everyone has a lot of work, and that's just how it is". As a result, there is a strong perception that those who set clear boundaries are less committed compared to colleagues who are constantly available. In this environment, psychological detachment is often misunderstood as laziness or a lack of work ethic, rather than recognised as an essential strategy for maintaining occupational wellbeing. And how has this been addressed at my school? With individual focused strategies or one-day "relaxation" activities like team building days. But these can feel like asking someone to run when they're already too tired! I don't think this has solved the problem at all. The real issue is the constant high pressure we face. This reality is slowly forcing us to recognise that the mindset needs to change.

This example highlights the intersection between psychosocial hazards and work-related recovery. If there is significant work overload, as described here, this will overwhelm the capacity of individuals to self-regulate. These opportunities for recovery need to occur daily and at work as well as at home (Chan et al., 2022).

> It is essential for school leadership and everyone involved to actively prioritise and support intentional recovery opportunities for teachers and staff without feeling guilty or making others feel guilty for doing so. Recovery should not be "a luxury"; it must be built into the flow of the workday. This includes practical steps such as providing a quiet room for breaks and leisure, offering flexible scheduling, and ensuring regular, structured breaks throughout the day.
>
> Leadership must also consider recovery strategies as an ongoing approach to staff wellbeing rather than treating them as one-day or

short-term solutions. This means protecting non-work time, such as weekends and holidays, by setting clear boundaries around work-related communication and expectations. And that, I believe, means working hard without life becoming hard!

As this middle leader highlights, the ability to recover from work is closely tied to leading practices and workplace arrangements rather than a solely individual responsibility. An early sign that demands are outstripping resources is the internal signal that we need to take a break. We often tend to ignore these signals, in a way that we wouldn't necessarily ignore physical symptoms if we were doing a physical task. And if we do ignore them, we tend to do so for long-term gain. For example, let's say we are doing a strength training program with weights. We will push ourselves a bit to increase muscle strength in the long term but not generally so far that we do ourselves an injury. People are often less aware and strategic about managing psychological effort than they are about managing physical effort, in part because the outcome is less clear. A demanding day at work can have a variety of effects, including fatigue, ruminating about work, tense muscles, a headache, stomach upset, irritability, and trouble sleeping (tired but wired). It is this lack of awareness and focus on our own wellbeing that we are trying to remedy here by providing a framework for long-term management of educators' working lives. If we wait until we're already burnt out, it is much harder to address, because burnout decreases proactive behaviour and effective coping (Pietarinen et al., 2021).

Job Crafting

Individual job crafting is a form of employee-driven job design which has been widely researched and shown to have positive effects on wellbeing and performance (Silapurem et al., 2024). Job crafting research comes from two research traditions: those based on Job Demands-Resources Theory (Tims et al., 2012) and those based on qualitative research from Wrzesniewski and Dutton (2001). Recent reviews have combined data on these two approaches and split job crafting into approach/promotion crafting and avoidance/prevention crafting (Bindl et al., 2019; Zhang & Parker, 2019).

The Theory of Planned Behaviour can be applied to job crafting and suggests that behaviour (in this case job crafting) is proceeded by an intention, and this intention is caused by the combination of three factors:

1. Attitude towards the behaviour – believing the consequences of the behaviour are worthwhile.
2. Social norms – believing those around them will approve of the behaviour.
3. Perceived behavioural control – believing they have the autonomy to perform the behaviour.

(Costantini et al., 2019)

Costantini et al. (2019) argue that we need to consider the cultural, social, and organisational context to successfully encourage job crafting. We can also see here the need for leaders to model, support, and allow autonomy for job crafting to occur productively.

The easiest way to start thinking about job crafting is to identify a time when you changed something at work. Take a moment to think about something you have changed – why did you make this change, and what was the outcome? The changes we make will generally fall into a few different categories. For example, you may have changed a meeting agenda to allow for discussion time (relational crafting), created a template for a common report (task crafting), or attended some extra training in an area of interest (resource crafting).

Resource-based crafting based on the Job Demands-Resources model (Tims et al., 2012) includes the following:

1 Reducing hindrances – such as simplifying a reporting process
2 Increasing challenges – such as taking on an extra role in something you are passionate about
3 Increasing structural resources – such as attending professional learning
4 Increasing social resources – such as asking for feedback or coaching

Role-based crafting based on the work of Wrzesniewski and Dutton (Wrzesniewski et al., 2013) includes the following:

1 Task crafting – such as creating a template for a regular report
2 Relational crafting – such as developing a relationship with someone outside your department who has a different approach to teaching
3 Cognitive crafting – such as taking a new perspective on something that you have found frustrating

Clearly, there is a lot of conceptual overlap in the categories above, but the main thing to keep in mind is that there are many ways of crafting our work each day, in both small and larger ways.

Practice Menu

Understanding leading as a practice can help you to understand how practices of leading pedagogy, learning, and wellbeing leading can be distributed amongst a team of leaders and how important teams and learning communities are for growth and wellbeing. The practices of Job crafting in the menu are a start to understanding your own role in leading learning and wellbeing as you relate to and work with others.

Current practices	Questions about practice arrangements	Suggested practices for application
Sayings (communication) Do I ask *what we need to do to work together better*? Do I ask people how they are going?	*Cultural-discursive arrangements* Do we talk about individual job crafting as we lead? Do we talk about how to recover from work?	Job Demands-Resources model (Tims et al., 2012) includes the following: 1 Reducing demands – such as simplifying a reporting process 2 Increasing challenges – such as taking on an extra role in something you are passionate about 3 Increasing structural resources – such as attending professional learning 4 Increasing social resources – such as asking for feedback or coaching
Doings Am I actively job crafting? Are we collaboratively job crafting in my team? Am I aware of my own work habits and intentions? Am I developing recovery habits?	*Material-economic arrangements* Are demands and resources balanced in my role? Are demands and resources balanced in our team?	
Relatings Am I engaged in work or burnt out? What opportunities do I have for autonomy, connection, and developing my capabilities?	*Social-political arrangements* Can we recognise motivation or burnout in our team? Am I supporting my team in autonomy, connection and competence? Do we consider how to reduce demands and increase collaboration?	Role-based crafting based on the work of Wrzesniewski and Dutton (Wrzesniewski et al., 2013) includes 1 Task crafting – such as creating a template for a regular report 2 Relational crafting – such as developing a relationship with someone outside your department who has a different approach to teaching 3 Cognitive crafting – such as taking a new perspective on something that you have found frustrating
*Dispositions (habitus)*Do I understand what motivates me?What are my levels of work engagement and burnout?	*Practice traditions* Do we distribute leadership amongst the leadership team? Do we encourage work recovery and breaks from work?	

Summary of Key Points

- 'What do we need' to work together? is a helpful question that enables leaders to identify the resources, demands, problems, and the practices needed to change their leading practices during change.
- Roles and tasks change all the time with the changing demands of schooling.

- Leaders need time to evaluate their work both alone and together.
- We all craft our individual roles, but we can do this more strategically.
- Job crafting is a practice of distributing leading. Teachers and leaders need to work together beyond distribution to ways of crafting their roles in accordance with the needs of their context and the key priority at the time.
- Collective job crafting is a way of doing what we value together.
- Sustainable workloads are possible through individual and collective job crafting, and this takes communication and action through a process.
- Recovery from work is also an integral aspect of work and workplace wellbeing.

References

Andrews, D., Conway, J., Dawson, M., Lewis, M., McMaster, J., Morgan, A., & Starr, H. (2004). *School Revitalisation the IDEAS way*. ACEL Monograph Series No. 34. Winmalee, NSW: Australian Council for Educational Leaders.

Bakker, A.B., & De Vries, J.D. (2021). Job demands–resources theory and self-regulation: New explanations and remedies for job burnout. *Anxiety, Stress, & Coping*, 34(1), 1–21.

Bindl, U.K., Unsworth, K.L., Gibson, C.B., & Stride, C.B. (2019). Job crafting revisited: Implications of an extended framework for active changes at work. *Journal of Applied Psychology*, 104(5), 605.

Blase, J., & Blase J. (1998). *Handbook of Instructional Leadership: How Really Good Principals Promote Teaching and Learning*. Thousand Oaks, CA: Corwin Press.

Chan, P.H.H., Howard, J., Eva, N., & Tse, H.H.M. (2022). A systematic review of at-work recovery and a framework for future research. *Journal of Vocational Behaviour*, 137, September. DOI:10.1016/j.jvb.2022.103747

Chew, J.O.A., & Andrews, D. (2010). Enabling teachers to become pedagogical leaders: Case studies of two IDEAS schools in Singapore and Australia. *Educational Research for Policy and Practice*, 9(1), 59–74.

Costantini, A., Ceschi, A., & Sartori, R. (2019). The theory of planned behaviour as a frame for job crafting: Explaining and enhancing proactive adjustment at work. In L. Van Zyl & S. Rothmann Sr. (Eds.), *Theoretical Approaches to Multi-Cultural Positive Psychological Interventions* (pp. 161–177). Singapore: Springer. doi:10.1007/978-3-030-20583-6_7

Day, C., & Armstrong, P. (2016). England: School leadership research in England. In H. Arlestig, C. Day, O. Johansson (Eds.), *A Decade of Research on School Principals: Cases from 24 Countries* (pp. 245–268). Singapore: Springer.

Edwards-Groves, C., Grootenboer, P., Petrie, K., & Nicholas, Z. (2022). Practising educational leading 'in' and 'from' the middle: A site ontological view of best practice. *Journal of Educational Administration and History*, 55(1), 72–88. DOI:10.1080/00220620.2022.2066637

English, F., & Ehrich, L.C. (2017). Disambiguating leadership: The continuing quest for the philosopher's stone. In G. Lakomski, S. Eacott & C. Evers (Ed.), *Questioning Leadership: New Directions for Educational Organisations* (pp. 3–16). New York: Routledge.

Grice, C. (2018). Leading pedagogical reform. *International Journal of Leadership in Education*, 22(3), 355–370. DOI:10.1080/13603124.2018.1463462

Grice, C. (2025). *The Practices of Leading Pedagogy*. Singapore: Springer.

Grice, C., Forssten Seiser, A., & Wilkinson, J. (2023). Decentring pedagogical leadership: Educational leading as a pedagogical practice. *Journal of Educational Administration and History*, 55(1), 89–107. DOI:10.1080/00220620.2022.2163381

Gronn, P. (2017). Commentary: Silo's bunkers and their voice. In G. Lakomski, S. Eacott and C. Evers (Ed.), *Questioning Leadership: New Directions for Educational Organisations* (pp. 192–202). New York: Routledge.

Grootenboer, P. (2018). *The Practices of School Middle Leadership: Leading Professional Learning*. Singapore: Springer.

Gurr, D., Drysdale, L., & Mulford, B. (2005). Successful principal leadership: Australian case studies. *Journal of Educational Administration*, 43(6), 539–551. DOI:10.1108/09578230510625647

Hall, D. (2013). The strange case of the emergence of distributed leadership in schools in England. *Educational Review*, 65(4), 467–487.

Harris, A. (2014). *Distributed Leadership Matters: Perspectives, Practicalities and Potential*. Thousand Oaks, CA: Corwin Sage.

Kemmis, S., Wilkinson, J., Edwards-Groves, C., Hardy, I., Grootenboer, P., & Bristol, L. (2014). *Changing Practices, Changing Education*. Singapore: Springer.

Lakomski, G., & Evers, C. (2017). In G. Lakomski, S. Eacott and C. Evers (Ed.), *Questioning Leadership: New Directions for Educational Organisations* (pp. 3–16). New York: Routledge.

Leithwood, K., Harris, A., & Hopkins, D. (2020). Seven strong claims about successful school leadership revisited. *School Leadership & Management*, 40(1), 5–22. DOI: 10.1080/13632434.2019.1596077

Pietarinen, J., Pyhältö, K., Haverinen, K., Leskinen, E., & Soini, T. (2021). Is individual- and school-level teacher burnout reduced by proactive strategies? *International Journal of School and Educational Psychology*, 9(4), 340–355. DOI:10.1080/21683603.2021.1942344

Roosevelt, T. n.d. *An Autobiography*, Chapter 9, accessed at https://standardebooks.org/ebooks/theodore-roosevelt/an-autobiography

Silapurem, L., Slemp, G.R., & Jarden, A. (2024). Longitudinal job crafting research: A meta-analysis. *International Journal of Applied Positive Psychology*, 9, 899–933. DOI:10.1007/s41042-024-00159-0

Sonnentag, S., Cheng, B.H., & Parker, S.L. (2022). Recovery from work: Advancing the field toward the future. *Annual Review of Organizational Psychology and Organizational Behavior*, 9(1), 33–60.

Spillane, J.P. (2006). *Distributed Leadership*. San Francisco, CA: Jossey Bass.

Tims, M., Bakker, A.B., & Derks, D. (2012). Development and validation of the job crafting scale. *Journal of Vocational Behavior*, 80(1), 173–186.

Tuerktorun, Y.Z., Weiher, G.M., & Horz, H. (2020). Psychological detachment and work-related rumination in teachers: A systematic review. *Educational Research Review*, 31, 100354.

Wenger, E. (1998). *Communities of Practice: Learning, Meaning and Identity*. Cambridge, UK: Cambridge University Press.

Wilkinson, J. (2017). Reclaiming education in educational leadership. In P. Grootenboer, C. Edwards-Groves, & S. Choy (Eds.), *Practice Theory Perspectives on Pedagogy and Education* (pp. 231–241). Singapore: Springer.

Wilkinson, J. (2021). *Educational Leadership through a Practice Lens: Practice Matters*. Singapore: Springer.

Wilkinson, J., & Kemmis, S. (2014). Practice theory: Viewing leadership as leading. *Educational Philosophy and Theory*, *47*(4), 342–358. DOI:10.1080/00131857.2014.976928

Wilkinson, J., Walsh, L., Keddie, A., & Longmuir, F. (2021). *Educational Leadership Through a Practice Lens: Practice Matters* In J. Wilkinson (Ed.), (pp. 157–183). 1st ed. (Educational Leadership Theory). Singapore: Springer.

Woods, P., & Roberts, A. (2019). Collaborative school leadership in a global society: A critical perspective. *Educational Management Administration & Leadership*, *47*(5), 663–677. DOI:10.1177/1741143218759088

Woods, P.A., & Roberts, A. (2015). Distributed leadership and social justice: Images and meanings from across the school landscape. *International Journal of Leadership in Education*, *19*(2), 138–156. DOI:10.1080/13603124.2015.1034185

Wrzesniewski, A., & Dutton, J.E. (2001) Crafting a job: Revisioning employees as active crafters of their work. *Academy of Management Review*, *25*, 179–201.

Wrzesniewski, A., LoBuglio, N., Dutton, J.E., & Berg, J.M. (2013). Job crafting and cultivating positive meaning and identity in work. In *Advances in Positive Organizational Psychology*, Vol. 1 (pp. 281–302). Bradford, UK: Emerald Group Publishing Limited.

Youngs, H. (2017). A critical exploration of collaborative and distributed leadership in higher education: Developing an alternative ontology through leadership-as-practice. *Journal of Higher Education Policy and Management*, *39*(2), 140–154. https://doi.org/10.1080/1360080X.2017.1276662

Zhang, F., & Parker, S.K. (2019). Reorienting job crafting research: A hierarchical structure of job crafting concepts and integrative review. *Journal of Organizational Behavior*, *40*(2), 126–146. DOI:10.1002/job.2332

6 Mastering the Practices of Leading Together

Collaboration, Capability

Leading together sounds great, but isn't it just too much work? And what is the real intention behind suggesting we collaborate? Leading together is a process, not just an outcome. This chapter gives suggestions about practices that are precursors to collaboration and enables them to evaluate whether they are collaborating, with collective thinking, sense-making, and action from sharing expertise, purpose, and values. Alternatively, are they being collaborators, or spies, influenced by prior experiences of coercion and control? The chapter provides specific ideas for improving everyday practices: what leaders can do and say and the interpersonal aspects of leadership. Research on collaboration shows that relationships and collective efficacy are important, and this chapter gives suggestions about how to build them. We suggest that collaboration is the key capability of a middle leader. When collaboration is aligned with purpose, everyone can be engaged in collective purpose.

Examples from Schools

Leading together is a process, not just an outcome. Bono, in his autobiography, Surrender (2022), explains collaboration as comradeship and creation where the individuals in the band multiply what they create themselves through the band, and that is its purpose. The best way to build collaborative relationships is through the interpersonal aspects of leadership and specifically through the practices of active listening, questioning, and encouraging conversation.

> Listening is important. I think it's a skill that you learn more about as a middle leader, but I think as an executive leader you understand a lot more the importance of listening – really active listening, engaging with the speaker, acknowledging what they're saying to you, and understanding. A lot of empathy that is needed, because you never know what's going to happen through problem solving. I think that's important that you put your pen down, phone down, computer down and listen because everybody's important and wants to be heard. There are some outstanding heads of department who have that ability to listen,

understand and develop their thoughts, and then draw decisions that then allow their teams to work together. I find middle leaders who allow for listening and encouraging others within their teams to make decisions are the ones that have the most impact on change. I think it's a skill that needs to be encouraged and developed further through open questioning techniques and encouraging conversation and active listening.

Active listening also sits beside activism for middle leaders because listening is demonstrated through action.

My role in supporting middle leaders is often as a sounding board to help them work through problems. I'm also there to directly represent their concerns at times when they feel they can't, to the senior leadership team. If they are not feeling safe to make their concerns known, then my support is vital for them. I see my support as just acting as a sounding board. Having their back, sharing the strategic vision of the school and developing it with them. Really listening to them. I try to represent their views. If they come to me and share concerns with me, I will put those concerns together in a way that protects their psychological safety. I don't name them or their departments. Its building the trust that they can come and see you about something and have a robust conversation and be able to make a joint decision on something that is for the benefit of everyone. When middle leaders have a voice, they have a sense of ownership, and they will take responsibility to then be able to make it happen.

Physical architectures can enable and constrain robust conversations, and yet communication in all directions is essential for the functioning of the school as well as a shared language.

Clear, frequent honest communication and meetings support the building of collaborative relationships. The biggest barrier is how physically distant the middle leaders are from each other on the school campus and how rarely they meet. We need a shared physical space where people come to regularly. Things like a morning tea sound like, we want food, we want to eat. We just need to see people. If the middle leaders saw more of each other instead of having to make quite a considerable journey or pick up a phone, those relationships would change. People don't really want to pick up a phone because it makes it very formal, intentional contact, rather than more informal, where you then discover that you have some shared ideas/concerns. If I am worried about something, or need to do something, getting up, walking out of my office, going across the school in whichever direction is necessary, to talk something through is important. Rather than shoot off an email, or just go, oh, well, that's the way it is. I think it's that making the effort to be in person to build those relationships, by going into their space, seeing where they are, and sharing with them.

Collaboration is the key capability of a middle leader. Collaborating involves collective thinking, sense-making, and action from sharing expertise, purpose, and values.

Communication skills build relationships and collaboration.

Their ability to collaborate with others and facilitate those relationships. Working with people, building relationships and maintaining effective relationships which may involve robust conversation, planning, being able to reach beyond, the small groups and to be able to support teachers in thinking and building relationships beyond smaller, academic groups or wellbeing spaces. They need to be good communicators. They need to be focused on relationships with staff, other colleagues, with their students, with parents, it's very relational. The most important part is how they communicate and collaborate with their team and make it a cohesive team that can be empowered to try new things, to give positive and negative feedback about what's happening in a really safe environment. If you feel empowered and connected and there is good communication, that's one of the secrets for middle contributing to change. Sometimes that's not always easy in a big school and I think being able to communicate more in their meetings with middle leaders is an essential part of it.

Middle leaders may be ready to collaborate, but if they lack agency across the school, the work they do together can be diminished.

Across teams there is not a sufficient opportunity to build capacity and to share concerns. The building of social capital, the regular participation in school-wide decision-making. The middle leaders lack agency at times because they're not consulted – they're told.

In contrast,

There was a group of middle leaders and staff that explored pilot projects last year. The middle leaders had an opportunity to ask questions and explore it together. They are leading and they've got complete agency over who's focusing on what.

Being strategic about collaboration and improvement through meeting structures is important for developing the relational work that builds a collective.

> We've put a lot of resourcing and time and effort and energy into moving towards that developing phase. We've put structures around what we're going to do. As an example, in 2021, we had a committee made up of leaders and teachers that were looking at how we create time for people to collaborate, to focus on improvement of their teaching and learning practice. At 8 o'clock every Monday morning, we had regular professional development time in our schedule of meetings devoted to developing leadership and developing our team.

The structured time can be beneficial, or it can look bureaucratic to middle leaders, depending on the level of agency they have with that information, which is also dependent on the disposition of a middle leader and not just their position.

Balancing confidentiality and surveillance is necessary so that middle leaders do not feel spied on, like collaborators (Grice, 2019), instead of collaborating together.

> Alongside my director, I work with six homeroom teachers who are the primary touchstone for the pastoral needs of students in our house. Our school utilises a typical bureaucratic structure meaning I am the midway point between the senior leadership team and the homeroom teachers. A large amount of crucial information – attendance, student mood, homework, socialisation – flows from these teachers to me, mostly in the form of chronicle entries on our learning management system. As far as face-to-face interactions with staff, they tend to occur during structured meeting times once a fortnight and revolve around either student needs or my intentions for establishing a shared house vision. I have come to realise that a lot of the communication is transactional: I am tagged in a chronicle note from a homeroom teacher that requires approval or an action, I tag a homeroom teacher in a chronicle note that requires action, I ask a teacher to perform an action that contributes to our shared house goals, or we interact in a formal setting with little space to move beyond the meeting agenda. It is rare for me to be conversing with a homeroom teacher without talking about a particular student or group of students. In each instance there are subtle, codified conditions to our interactions which create a relationship predicated on monitoring. I have no doubt this could also be construed as a form of surveillance. There is a degree of inevitability here seeing as my role is regularly governed by procedural necessities and safeguarding policies. However, I can see that a professional relationship founded on interactions like this is going to have negative relations to basic needs satisfaction, generating less effective motivational processes and outcomes. Also, I am sure some of the additional pressure I feel by viewing my role through perceived threats is subconsciously passed on. My move towards external regulation can also have an impact on my team.

Connecting Research and Practice

In the movie, "Thor: Ragnarök", the ironic statement "We're a team" is said by Thor to Hulk and Loki after they have been captured by the Grandmaster and forced to participate in a gladiator tournament. In that moment, it is obvious to Thor and to the audience that they are not a team, because Thor has all the strength, power, and influence and is incapable of sharing. The movie captures the contemporary cynicism evident today in many workplaces where people are told to do teamwork, and yet the structures, people, and arrangements make this difficult or, in this case, ridiculous. It is not possible to change the strengths and talents of individuals. What can be changed is alignment to shared purpose. Thor, Hulk, and Loki started working together despite having very different strengths, once they knew that their purposes were aligned.

When collaboration is aligned with purpose, everyone can engage in collective purpose. Collaboration is a process of working together with shared purpose and expertise (Henneman et al., 1995; Ainscow et al., 2006; John-Steiner et al., 1998). In addition, people are committed to sharing and using their expertise in action (Cilliers, 2000), based on a shared understanding of how they need to work together in practice successfully (Campbell, 2021).

Ainscow, Muijs, and West (2006) critique the frequent use of collaborative mechanisms and suggest that collaboration involves moving from independent thinking and autonomy to collective thinking and action. We agree that collective thinking is essential but that being a collective should not have to mean a loss of autonomy. Mutual respect comes from shared autonomy. However, this is rarely the case, and collaboration has been seen by Datnow (2018) as increasing teacher stress and workload. Campbell (2024) critiques the lack of understanding of the intrinsic complexity of collaboration amongst educators despite its overuse in policy. When collaboration is captured by neoliberal policy discourse, it can take on different meanings, such as the spy or collaborator (Grice, 2019) who ensures compliance. Taking this into account, collaboration as a concept and in practice requires a commitment to analysing how individuals interact, connect, and make sense of the initiatives they engage in together and how they are influenced by prior experiences and interpretations of them (Wenger, 1998).

Hargreaves and Fullan write about professional capital as collaboration (2012), as a practice that supports teachers to build education that makes a difference. Capital is something you invest in that adds value. Professional capital is where teaching is seen as technically difficult, requiring shared expertise through collaboration for wise judgment. This gives school educators time to reflect, discuss, and develop judgment over time, driven by capability and moral purpose.

Leading education collectively means fostering a collaborative and shared approach to leadership, where everyone, including students, teachers, and administrators, contributes to decision-making and problem-solving, aiming for a culture of shared growth and improvement. Walker and Riordan (2010) write about building collective relationships within culturally diverse staff groups where "the development of collective capacity among teachers in schools leads to improvements in teaching and learning and decision making in schools which in turn directly impact student learning outcomes" (p. 54). Conway (2008) explores the collective intelligence of teachers in schools in meaning-making as part of the IDEAS (Innovative Designs for Enhancing Achievements in Schools) project as leaders decide on their schoolwide pedagogy. Shaked and Schechter (2017) write about the collective wisdom of practice through professional learning to collective inquiry. Van Manen (1991) considers these to be pedagogical reflection and writes:

> All these forms of reflection regularly make up the life we live with children: (1) Anticipatory reflection enables us to deliberate about possible alternatives, decide on courses of action, plan the kinds of things we need to do, and anticipate the experiences we and others may have because of expected events or of our planned actions. Anticipatory reflection helps us to approach situations and other people in an organized, decision-making, prepared way. (2) Active or interactive reflection, sometimes called reflection- in-action, allows us to come to terms with the situation or problem with which we are immediately confronted. This stop and- think type of reflection permits us to make decisions virtually on the spur of the moment. (3) There is also a common experience composed of the interactive pedagogical moment itself, characterized by a different type of reflectivity: a certain mindfulness. It is this mindfulness that distinguishes the interaction of tactful pedagogues from the other forms of acting.
>
> (p. 101)

van Manen (1991) suggests that reflection is the ultimate practice of a professional educator, not necessarily for problem-solving but to *be* pedagogical (p. 107), because the decisions that educators make have numerous predicaments and possibilities, in *pedagogical situations* (p.108) that occur rapidly and constantly throughout the day, lesson, or teaching moment. Collaboration has a positive impact on student experiences and attainment (Ainscow et al., 2011; Campbell, 2020).

Leading in Practice

Mastering the practices of leading together is essential, particularly for middle leaders where collaboration is their key capability. We provide several practice suggestions below. The chapter has raised a number of tensions for school leaders about collaboration. It is important for school leaders to consider how they might build trust in a context where surveillance is structurally embedded in schools to support learning. How can leaders balance issues of transparency with confidentiality in collaborative spaces when considering student wellbeing? Leaders carry these tensions in their work and they can impact collaboration.

Active Listening

Active listening, as mentioned above, is a practice that supports collaboration. There are many protocols that support active listening (Wasserman, 2017). "Circle of Voices" is a brainstorming technique that encourages participation in group conversation and listening. It is a small-group discussion technique designed to encourage participation from all members. In a "Circle of Voices" activity, participants take turns to share their initial thoughts or responses to a question or issue. This activity is based in Kolb and Kolb's (2018) experiential learning circles. The group is given a topic to discuss. First, individuals are given a few minutes to prepare their thinking before they start talking. A timed discussion begins where individuals have up to 2 minutes of uninterrupted talking time to share their viewpoint. During this time, no one else is allowed to say anything. This method helps gather consensus from the whole group, ensuring that all perspectives are heard. It also disciplines people to actively listen to each other, and teachers can find listening more challenging than speaking! Brookfield and Preskill (2016) have 50 protocols to choose from to encourage discussion with your team.

Meeting Protocols

Meeting protocols can also support collaboration and shared decision-making as well as project action. This includes pre-meeting preparation like creating an agenda and distributing it, note-taking, and following established rules during the meeting, such as arriving on time, actively listening, and respecting different perspectives. Connection and celebration during meetings are healthy ways of building a collaborative culture. At one school we worked with, the team would clap at the end of the meeting to celebrate the work they did together.

> After each executive meeting we clap. And there's a real positivity when we're talking about initiatives and things that middle leaders have say done together or initiatives across the school, it's all very positive. And then people are very keen to get involved, to have their say. No-one kind of sits back. People feel confident, and again, back to that relational trust, confident in having that input of what they think.

This simple gesture was done sincerely and created positivity and teamwork.

Project Initiatives

Another way of supporting collaboration between middle leaders is inviting them to think of interdisciplinary projects that they could work on together, be that across key stages or between different subject departments. This could lead to further professional learning for middle leaders as they lead initiatives.

Socratic Questioning

Socratic questioning is a method where a leader asks probing questions to guide people towards deeper understanding and fosters critical thinking during a meeting or professional learning session (Walker & Riordan, 2010). In this way, it increases the learning and questioning capacity of the group, through dialogue. Participants are invited to ask clarification questions such as *What do you mean by that? Can you give me an example?* Assumption questions: *What assumptions are you making? Is there a different point of view?* Probing questions: *What evidence supports your claim? What are the implications of this? and* alternative viewpoint questions such as *Are there other ways to look at this?* Participants are encouraged to examine their own beliefs, assumptions, and reasoning, through analysis rather than simply providing answers during sessions (Neenan, 2008). Deep thinking and responding support team-building through shared understanding and ownership. It can involve role play.

Socratic questioning follows the steps below, outlined by Sutton (2020).

1. Understand the belief. Ask the person to state clearly their belief/argument.
2. Sum up the person's argument. Play back what they said to clarify your understanding of their position.
3. Ask for evidence. Ask open questions to elicit further knowledge and uncover assumptions, misconceptions, inconsistencies, and contradictions. Ask: Upon what assumption is this belief based? What evidence is there to support this argument?
4. Challenge their assumptions. If contradictions, inconsistencies, exceptions, or counterexamples are identified, then ask the person to either disregard the belief or restate it more precisely.
5. Repeat the process, if required. Until both parties accept the restated belief, the process is repeated.

The order may not always proceed as above. However, the steps provide insight into how the questioning could proceed. Repeat the process to drill down into the core of an issue, thought, or belief.

Practice Menu

Current practices	Questions about practice arrangements	Suggested practices for application
Sayings (communication) Do I communicate clearly? Do I mainly instruct or invite?	*Cultural-discursive arrangements* Do we practice active listening skills and collaborative reflection to seek each other's views? Do we have honest conversations?	Mastering the practices of leading together is essential, particularly for middle leaders where collaboration is their key capability. Active listening is a practice that supports collaboration. There are many protocols that support active listening. Circle of Voices is a brainstorming technique that encourages participation in group conversation and listening. Meeting protocols can also support collaboration and shared decision-making as well as project action. Another way of supporting collaboration between middle leaders is inviting them to think of interdisciplinary projects that they could work on together, be that across key stages or between different subject departments. This could lead to further professional learning. Socratic questioning also supports team-building.
Doings Am I competent and knowledgeable about my role? Do I delegate/dump/plan to share?	*Material-economic arrangements* Do we delegate/dump/plan to share? Are we a knowledge learning team?	
Relatings Do I grow leadership in others?	*Social-political arrangements* Do we work well when the principal/senior/middle leader is absent? Are we growing shared, collaborative leadership across our team?	
Dispositions (habitus) Am I a hero/martyr? Do I seek/share the glory?	*Practice traditions* Do we share leading learning?	

Summary of Key Points

- Relationships and collective efficacy are important, and they are built by the habits of leading together. Habits become the practices that lead to working together.
- We work best together when working on tasks with shared purpose.
- When people do not have shared purpose, collaborating may look more like spying, coercing, or controlling.

- Collective job crafting supports the development of collaboration and engagement in work that supports wellbeing.
- Active listening, meeting protocols, Socratic questioning, and project initiatives are all practices that can support the shared purpose required for genuine collaboration.

References

Ainscow, M., Muijs, D., & West, M. (2006). Collaboration as a strategy for improving schools in challenging circumstances. *Improving Schools*, *9*(3), 192–202. DOI:10.1177/1365480206069014

Ainscow, M., & Miles, S. (2011). *Responding to Diversity in Schools*. London: Routledge.

Bono (2022). *Surrender: 40 Songs One Story*. London: Penguin.

Brookfield, S.D., & Preskill, S. (2016). *The Discussion Book. 50 Great Ways to Get People Talking*. Hoboken, NJ: Jossey-Bass.

Campbell, P. (2020). Rethinking professional collaboration and agency in a post-pandemic era. *Journal of Professional Capital and Community*, *5*(3/4), 337–341. DOI:10.1108/JPCC-06-2020-0033

Campbell, P. (2021). *Collaboration: The Ubiquitous Panacea for Challenges in Education*. EdD dissertation. University of Glasgow. https://theses.gla.ac.uk/82883/

Campbell, P. (2024). Conceptualising collaboration for educational change: the role of leadership and governance. *School Leadership & Management*, *44*(4), 347–372. doi: 10.1080/13632434.2024.2355469

Cilliers, P. (2000). Knowledge, complexity, and understanding. *Emergence*, *2*(4), 7–13. DOI: 10.1207/S15327000EM0204_03

Conway, J.M. (2008). *Collective Intelligence in Schools: An Exploration of Teacher Engagement in the Making of Significant New Meaning*. PhD dissertation. University of Southern Queensland.

Datnow, A. (2018). Time for change? The emotions of teacher collaboration and reform. *Journal of Professional Capital and Community*, *3*(3), 157–172. DOI: 10.1108/JPCC-12-2017-0028

Grice, C. (2019). 007 Spies, surveillance and pedagogical middle leadership: For the good of the empire of education. *Journal of Educational Administration and History*, *51*(2), 165–181. DOI: 10.1080/00220620.2019.1583173

Hargreaves, A., & Fullan, M. (2012). *Professional Capital: Transforming Teaching in Every School*. New York: Teachers College Press.

Henneman, E., Lee, J.N., & Cohen, J. (1995). Collaboration: A concept analysis. *Journal of Advanced Nursing*, *21*(1): 103–109. DOI:10.1046/j.1365-2648.1995.21010103.x

John-Steiner, V., Weber, R.J., & Minnis, M. (1998). The challenge of studying collaboration. *American Educational Research Journal*, *35*(4), 773–783. DOI:10.3102/00028312035004773

Kolb, A., & Kolb, D. (2018). Eight important things to know about the experiential learning cycle. *Australian Educational Leader*, *40*(3), 8–14.

Neenan, M. (2008). Using Socratic questioning in coaching. *Journal of Rational-Emotive & Cognitive-Behavior Therapy*, *27*(4), 249–264. DOI:10.1007/s10942-007-0076-z

Shaked, H., & Schechter, C. (2017). *Systems Thinking for School Leaders: Holistic Leadership for Excellence in Education*. Cham, Switzerland: Springer.

Sutton, J. (2020). Socratic questioning in psychology: Examples and techniques. Accessed at https://positivepsychology.com/socratic-questioning/

van Manen, M. (1991). *The Tact of Teaching: The Meaning of Pedagogical Thoughtfulness*. New York: State University of New York Press.

Walker, A., & Riordan, G. (2010). Leading collective capacity in culturally diverse schools. *School Leadership & Management*, 30(1), 51–63. DOI:10.1080/13632430903509766

Wasserman, S. (2017). *The Art of Interactive Teaching: Listening, Responding, Questioning* (1st ed.). New York: Routledge.

Wenger, E. (1998). *Communities of Practice: Learning, Meaning, and Identity*. Cambridge, UK: Cambridge University Press. DOI:10.1017/CBO9780511803932

7 Leading Together

Solidarity and Purpose from Collective Agency and Autonomy*

How intentional are you in your daily work? How intentional are others? This chapter is about authentically involving everyone in pedagogy, learning, and wellbeing. Self-Determination Theory (SDT) is a framework for encouraging leading and all teachers and leaders to be actively participating in school improvement. By tapping into the intrinsic motivation of students, teachers, and leaders and connecting work with purpose, leaders can foster autonomous motivation. A wide range of international research suggests that SDT applies across cultures, although there may be differences in the importance or strength of different needs. Given that this is about relationships, we wish to highlight Aboriginal perspectives on leading, learning, and wellbeing as integral to educating, and we take a perspective of cultural humility in learning from the insights of Aboriginal educators and colleagues where being grounded on country is connected with purpose. Where agency brings individual engagement and motivation, autonomy in the framework of SDT is a sense of volition and choice of how to act, not just for yourself but for community, with others. Leaders come together in solidarity and shared purpose by inviting leadership teams to consider their shared values, connected expertise, and commitment together.

Examples from Schools

Sara Kubric, author and millennial therapist, famously said: "Authenticity will take you places where people pleasing can't" (2025). People-pleasing seems to form many interactions in schools, and yet we are most motivated by being authentic and intentional as these examples from schools demonstrate.

At Xavier School, we explore ways that educators are actively involved in their daily work in wellbeing and learning practices. We explore multiple alternative perspectives of leading pedagogy and demonstrate how educators in schools utilise their internal sense of volition and choice in their practices, to know how to act. Autonomy can be enabled and spread or constrained and even crushed by executive leaders in a school. This can be caused by cultural, logistical, or

---

* This chapter was coauthored by Tarunna Sebastian, Michelle Donelly, and the primary authors.

DOI: 10.4324/9781003564843-8

leadership factors. When individuals within a team are each valued, collective solidarity of purpose builds a coherent whole. Solidarity of purpose comes through the following practices outlined below from school leaders themselves:

Leading pedagogy is about being intentional. A middle leader shares:

> Next year I am taking on a new position at my school, moving from a wellbeing role to one in teaching and learning. My new responsibilities include developing and implementing a future-focused learning vision that is grounded in creativity, innovation and forward thinking. and providing students with the skills and knowledge to access the world beyond the classroom. Currently the role involves working with the Director of Teaching and Learning and Heads of Departments to design cross-curricular opportunities for students. In the past these opportunities have generally come in the form of projects, assessments, and lesson activities. While the overarching vision for the role fits within a paradigm of lifelong learning, it neglects to conceptualise pedagogy as an all-encompassing practice beyond instruction: the practices that occur in the cultural-discursive and material-economic dimensions are prioritised over those in the social-political dimension. There is a greater focus on what teachers and students do and say rather than the way they relate to their work and each other. An example of this is that the success of programs, assessments, and resources are measured by the physical products produced – no evaluation tool considers the relational dynamics. This subconsciously promotes an instructional perception of pedagogy that limits opportunities for connectedness and solidarity. The practices that are related to my new role, especially ones that involve staff and students, need to be more considerate of the broader social arrangements within the school. There also needs to be a more purposeful way of understanding the relational byproducts of the existing 'sayings' and 'doings', as well as the voice of those involved. An incredible amount of power can be generated when there is coherence amongst the practices and the established paradigm. I want to lead a pedagogical change that better recognises the relational practices that occur in the school and intentionally orchestrates more opportunities for them. Recognising pedagogy as present across all dimensions leads to a more coherent understanding of the ecology of a school site. Acknowledging and deliberately facilitating opportunities for staff to connect in the social space contributes positively to the wellbeing of all participants, particularly teachers. Agency and voice are cornerstones to any sustainable relationship and play a crucial role in building a democratically responsive paradigm like lifelong learning.

Solidarity comes from understanding your vision and direction together:

> I think middle leaders need to have a vision. It's also ensuring that they're drawn into creating a shared vision and understanding and direction together. It's not being done to them, but we're walking alongside and supporting the middle leaders to have a shared vision and direction of where we're going.

Building trust involves caring for others, enabling collegiality, risk-taking, and trust-building.

> You can bring a cultural shift over time, but that takes a long time for people to trust you and that you mean what you say. And that what you're doing is authentic and that it's going to continue. When you feel that you are trusted, when you feel that you are cared for, when you feel that yes, I can make mistakes because there's someone there, you know to help you. It's working together. It's supporting each other and we know we make mistakes. We learn from them, we grow. We're trying to create an attitude shift that we can all work together by using the expertise of the whole team rather than just the some that want to be involved.

Creating a safe space enables voice. Disagreements will happen, and people will learn how to solve them together.

> Our Senior Executive team, even with disagreements, remain extremely professional and try and keep open about the reason for doing things. We try and make sure our whole team has agency. That was something that we tried to create early on. One of the reasons why we went down this path came from a brief conversation we had in the executive meeting. A couple of people were misrepresented and it became a whole big thing in the background that we weren't aware of. The issue was brought back to us in a completely different form saying that we were imposing on people when we hadn't even discussed the issue. So, we thought, how has this come about? At that point we asked, how do we stop this from happening between us?

Agency breeds autonomy.

> I feel like I have credibility and agency in an executive meeting. And I feel confident that when we discuss a topic or when I pitch or launch an idea, I am confident about the buy-in that I have from staff. We've now have an hour at the start of each meeting for executive collaboration time with middle leaders. The intention is to focus on a driving question and to pitch ideas and debate points. We want to hear from our middle leaders. We want to know their opinions. We've created such a safe space in that environment that I'm seeing middle leaders who sat there for two years without saying something, now speaking up. That gives me confidence that they feel like they have the agency in that room.
> We've restructured our meetings to have more of that collaboration time where we discuss teaching and learning and professional learning and provide opportunities for middle leaders to work together to really give their input. It's been received well. It's been in place for a while now. And you have enabled for that to happen I believe at our school. And

there's a huge focus on not just transparency but a consultative approach to anything that we are looking at implementing or changing. I wouldn't say we have all the head teachers on the same page all the time, I am realistic like that. I know that's not the case.

Vision comes from values. For Aboriginal people, this happens with Elders on Country.

> Uncle Ben is our local Elder, and he is also a key mentor and powerful source of guidance and leadership. His influence on me has been profound, especially during our staff development sessions held on Country with him. Although he left school early, Uncle Ben demonstrates deep, visionary leadership. He plays a significant role in our school community, walking alongside staff and students with generosity, humility, and cultural strength.

Being an educator is a giving practice.

> Teaching, to me, is a practice of giving. I have always wanted to be a teacher, and that desire has never wavered. I see the impact it has, not only on students, but on families, the broader Community, and even on my own growth.

Aboriginal leaders are the voice for their community, addressing the challenges faced by Aboriginal students and teachers. They act as mentors and advocates for policies and programs. In this way, leadership is not about a role but about strengths that come from autonomy.

> Aboriginal leadership is grounded in voice, advocacy, and relational responsibility. It's not limited to holding a formal position. Instead, it comes from strength, lived experience, and the commitment to stand up for Community. It's about walking in ways that uphold culture, connection, and care.
>
> My mum and my Aunties are incredible educators within our community. Because of the barriers they faced, they didn't have the chance to be recognised formally, but they have taught me more than any system could. When they see me stepping into spaces they were once excluded from, they carry pride in that journey. And I carry them with me.
>
> There are so many people in our community with different strengths and stories. Leadership isn't just about a role, it's about how we move through the world with purpose. Many of our people lead without ever being named as leaders. That's why it's so important that we value the strengths of everyone and understand that we each play a role in shaping the future together.

When people feel seen and heard, when their voices are respected, healing becomes possible. We can begin to mend the harm carried by our families and ancestors by creating space for connection, support, and cultural renewal, however that looks and feels right for each person.

For me, leadership is grounded in a holistic understanding—seeing the interconnections between people, practices, places, and histories. It's about walking together without judgement, learning from one another, and giving what we can to strengthen our children and our communities. That's the kind of leadership I hope to carry forward.

As Aboriginal educators think about their roles and responsibilities and how to make things better, they engage in self-reflection about

how they can strengthen and refine their teaching practice, deepen and expand their resources, particularly in relation to Aboriginal pedagogies and knowledges, improve student engagement, respond to classroom challenges, navigate growing administrative pressures, manage budget responsibilities, and sustain themselves amidst increasing workload demands.

Aboriginal cultures place great importance on the preservation, revival, and transmission of traditional knowledge, where Ancestral wisdom, stories, and practices remain accessible and relevant within a contemporary educational context. For Aboriginal students, seeing their culture reflected positively in the classroom in inclusive ways can have a profound impact on their self-identity and self-esteem. It exposes all students, regardless of their cultural backgrounds, to Aboriginal perspectives and knowledge, fostering an appreciation of diversity and multiculturalism. Furthermore, Aboriginal pedagogies and knowledges often contain traditional stories, languages, and practices that are vital for cultural preservation. Aboriginal teachers play a crucial role in passing down this cultural heritage to future generations.

Wildwood Forest School is about intentional "uncoerced learning". Wildwood provides the time, the site, the tools and the animals for learning… the rest is up to the kids. As Einstein said, 'I do not teach anyone, I only provide the environment in which they learn'. If you ever get the chance to witness learning in the wild, as in, learning without coercion, then you might see that it moves in a very different rhythm to the factory stuff. Factory learning expects a certain regularity to its pace. It seems to assume that there is only so much learning one can 'achieve' in a day and then on the flip side that opportunities for daydreaming and zoning out must be strictly reserved for special 'non-learning' hours. The reality of un-coerced learning seems to be very different. Wild learning moves very slowly for a time. Gently testing, poking and tentatively dipping toes into many different pools. Then all of sudden, whoosh! It picks up and gathers a breathtaking amount of speed. Consuming all available content as furiously as possible, repeating new facts, sharing exciting discoveries with any half-interested victim and defiantly ignoring normal sleeping patterns.... then one day, almost without warning the pace drops back to a slow trot, then a dawdle, sometimes even a complete stop. And from the outside it looks like the learning has stopped. At our weaker moments we may even be tempted to believe that laziness has taken over. Like they somehow despise the thought of 'fast paced' learning. But nevertheless, with enough space and freedom to explore, the curiosity will be sparked, and the cycle will repeat itself again... and again and again. Leaving a beautiful trail of half-finished projects and new-found wonder at the remarkable world that God has given us.

(Tom Batty)

At Wildwood Forest School, children learn how to contribute, negotiate, and compromise and to accept disappointment. Children are accepted regardless of what they can and can't do, and giving approval is avoided. They learn by doing. "Self-directed means that we provide the resources, and the kids bring the ideas."

Connecting Research and Practice

Self-Determination Theory

Motivation was first used to describe the reasons for human behaviour in the late 19th Century and was rarely used until the 1950s, although its use has escalated since then (Oxford University Press, n.d.). Research on motivation is extensive, and many articles have been published since 2000. We often talk about motivation both in education and in the workplace, including judging ourselves or others in relation to it. For example, "they are lazy" or "why can't I get myself moving?" But what is motivation, and how do we understand it?

In everyday use, we tend to think of motivation as something that is inherent within an individual – "she is motivated, he is not". We often also think of motivation as having a quantity – "they are highly motivated", "their motivation is low". This accords with one of the dictionary definitions of motivation: "desire or willingness to do something; enthusiasm" (Oxford University Press, n.d.). Even the example given in the Oxford Dictionary is telling in terms of our everyday understanding: "keep staff up to date and maintain interest and motivation".

We don't often think of motivation as having a quality or a context – that is, that some types of motivation might be better than others or that environment might make a difference. These ideas are more clearly linked to the other definition of motivation: "a reason or reasons for acting or behaving in a particular way" (Oxford University Press, n.d.). This use is closer to the origin of motivation – from motive ("a reason for doing something") and motivate ("provide (someone) with a reason for doing something") (Oxford University Press, n.d.).

When we do think about it in this way we often think about compliance – using rewards and punishments to "motivate" someone to behave as we want. But is this what we want for ourselves? Does this help us to thrive as human beings?

Self-Determination Theory (SDT) is one of the major theories of motivation and provides a useful framework for thinking about motivation in both students and educators. In SDT, there is a basic assumption that individuals are oriented toward growth and that the right environment will support them to thrive (Ryan et al., 2021; Ryan et al., 2022). One of the basic tenets of SDT is that when people's actions are self-determined, the long-term outcomes will be better, and there is strong research evidence that this is the case (Ryan et al., 2022). SDT has been studied in many different cultural contexts worldwide, including Indigenous Australians (Magson et al., 2024), China (Yu et al., 2018), India and Nigeria (Sheldon et al., 2009), and Mexico, Venezuela, the Philippines, Malaysia, and Japan (Church et al., 2013), to name just a few. This research suggests that the basic principles hold but may be expressed in different ways or vary in terms of strength (Van den Broeck et al., 2016).

Controlled and Autonomous Motivation

The major distinction in SDT is between controlled and autonomous motivation (Deci et al., 2017). Controlled motivations are those imposed by others (rewards and punishments, carrots and sticks) as well as those we impose on ourselves in response (such as punishing ourselves through guilt or performing from anxiety). Research has shown that this type of motivation is not conducive to performance or wellbeing (Deci et al., 2017). This makes sense – if you are doing something only to gain an external reward or to avoid a punishment, as soon as these external motivators are gone, so is the motivation. For example, think about students left alone in a classroom – will they be quiet and do their work, or will they talk?

There are two different types of autonomous motivations. The most important one for students (particularly when young) is intrinsic motivation – this is where we do something because doing it is fun or interesting (such as play) (Deci et al., 2017). This is the type of motivation we feel when we are pursuing a hobby or reading a book from our favourite author. It is often experienced as relatively effortless. As we get older, internalised extrinsic motivation increases in importance. This is when we do something with choice and willingness because it is in line with our values, we believe it is important or meaningful, or because it aligns with our goals or how we see ourselves as a person (Deci et al., 2017). An example would be the artist who works at a café, not because they want to but because the income allows them to pursue their art. Or the educator who takes extra time with assignment feedback, not because they enjoy it but because they believe it is important to student learning which is something that they value. Both types of autonomous motivations are important at work and contribute to our performance, work satisfaction, and wellbeing.

Basic Psychological Needs

When people's basic psychological needs are met at work, they are more likely to experience autonomous (or self-determined) motivations (Deci et al., 2017). The three basic psychological needs in SDT are autonomy, belonging (or relatedness), and competence (Deci et al., 2017). Autonomy refers to our perception that we can choose our actions. Belonging refers to our perception that we are valued by others. And competence refers to our belief in our capabilities in a situation. There are significant amounts of research showing that these ideas apply in educational settings to both students and teacher (Ryan et al., 2022). For example, autonomous motivation in teachers predicts both positive wellbeing outcomes for teachers and autonomy-supportive teaching (Slemp et al., 2020).

Using autonomy as an example, we might have two people who are doing their job for the income and have little job involvement. They are both doing their job for extrinsic reasons – not because they enjoy it. Person A may feel that they have no choice – other jobs are unavailable, and they need to pay their bills. Person A is motivated for external reasons. Person B has chosen a low-stress job close to home that allows them to spend time with their family, which is what they value. Person B has an internal motivation for their work – even if that motivation isn't the work itself. If we think about the consequences of this, Person A will likely do the minimum needed to keep their job, while Person B will more likely value keeping their job because of the other benefits.

Belonging refers to a sense of being valued as part of a social group and being in positive relationships with others. There is growing research on the importance of student belonging to student wellbeing and academic performance (Korpershoek et al., 2020). Similarly, we can see that social relationships are also critical to educator wellbeing (Zhou et al., 2024).

Competence is about our sense of self-efficacy – feeling as if we can meet the challenges of our environment and learn new skills (Van den Broeck et al., 2016). If we are required to do something but we have no idea how to do it or don't have the resources to do it, our motivation will take a hit. Procrastination is one common outcome of this scenario, which is then often perceived by us and others as laziness or poor performance. In schools, this might be the student with undiagnosed dyslexia who is struggling to read or the new teacher who is struggling with a challenging student cohort because they are still developing classroom management skills.

Self-Determination Theory at Work

If we assume that "behaviour is communication", SDT is helpful because it allows us to identify what type of motivation we are experiencing and understand what is affecting our motivation, and it suggests ways to move forward. For example, we may identify that we are putting off a work task, realise that we are anxious about completing it due to concerns that we don't know what standard is required, and then ask for help to clarify the requirements. Or we may wonder why a student is not completing work and ask them what is getting in the way of their engagement with the task. Do they know what to do? Do they have the skills? Do they see the point of the task? Is there a different way of approaching the work that might be more interesting or fun for them? Is there anyone they could work with who would help them feel like part of things?

We may experience more than one type of motivation at work – such as controlled motivation for administrative work and intrinsic motivation in the classroom. We may also experience more than one type of motivation for the same task – motivation for marking assessments can be intrinsic (for students who are progressing), internalised (seeing feedback as a tool for student learning), and external (we are paid to do it).

Leaders can influence motivation through the satisfaction of psychological needs in workplaces, particularly through autonomy-supportive practices (Slemp et al., 2018). Autonomy-supportive practices are associated with improved outcomes such as autonomous motivation and performance (Slemp et al., 2018). Recent research on need supportive leadership in an educational context suggests that it has positive effects (Collie, 2023). Autonomy-supportive practices include participative practices and attuning practices, while autonomy thwarting practices involve controlling practices that force compliance or domineering practices that generate feelings of shame or guilt (Collie, 2023).

Aboriginal Perspectives on Leading

The concept of Aboriginal leadership is difficult to understand when viewed through the non-Indigenous cultural lens because the practice is deeply related to the diverse contexts in which it occurs, including the values, traditions, and customs relevant to each Aboriginal Nation and its Communities. As Bill Ivory (2009) explains, Aboriginal people's notions of leadership clash with white concepts of leadership, and conflict will always arise when Aboriginal people are expected to conform to the latter. Aboriginal middle leaders work in a school environment which is largely determined by settler-colonial worldviews. Western/European/mainstream/dominant/settler-colonial worldviews are terms used interchangeably. They refer to structures that are predominantly capitalist, individualistic, and outcomes-driven and are shaped by the dominant ideology reflecting Western values, beliefs, and attitudes. This study looks at the education system in New South Wales that is based on dominant Western values. The notions of who is qualified to teach or lead and who is not, what is taught, and how it is taught reinforce dominant Western structures and capabilities. Furthermore, if not interrogated and challenged, these assumptions will perpetuate power imbalances between those with qualifications and positions of power and those without. The dominant worldviews are transmitted through schools' daily routines, strategies, structure, policies, processes, rewards, and control systems (Apple, 1988; Apple & Weiss, 1983; Giroux & McLaren, 1992). To make sense of the contemporary context of Australian middle leaders' experiences and Aboriginal education, it is helpful to understand the ongoing social, cultural, historical, and political impacts of these worldviews and how they continue to play out in schools.

Western constructs of 'leadership' and 'leader' are alien to Aboriginal peoples – there is no translatable word for these terms in Aboriginal languages. Broadly speaking, leadership is not a right or an individual choice in Aboriginal society (Morphy, 2007). Rather, leadership is often seen as a role granted or entrusted to an individual by others in their Community, Nation, school, or organisation. Furthermore, individuals become leaders not by self-appointment but through the acknowledgment and recognition of their leadership qualities and abilities by others. The skills of listening to others, working with cultural laws, and uniting Community are especially valued (Oscar, 2018). Oscar (2018, p. 1) goes further in defining Aboriginal leadership:

> Embedded within [our cultural] values are intrinsic lessons of our complex Kinship structures and cultural practices. These teach us of collective leadership, collaborative and inclusive decision-making, negotiation and cooperation, the reciprocal sharing of resources, life-long education, and the foundational understanding that an individual's health and wellbeing is intimately attached to the health of our country, our surrounding environments, and our families and Communities.

Within this collectivist and relational leadership framework, Aboriginal people often experience discomfort by being labelled or called a leader. Additionally, what is valued, categorised, and recognised within the Western leadership framework is at odds with the collective and relational nature of Aboriginal Law and governance systems (Jordan & Leroy-Dyer, 2023). Intergenerational ways of knowing, doing, and being are revitalised and passed down by the Elders to the school leaders, young children, and youth in schools, who can bond over stories of Kinship as well as our relationship with natural systems of law. Aboriginal cultures are dynamic, adaptive, and adapting, not limited to the past.

This Western worldview is characterised by individualism, rationalism, materialism, and humanism. The dominant Western leadership structure within educational institutions may favour Aboriginal middle leaders who conform to Western leadership models. However, this bias can limit the representation of Indigenous leaders in decision-making roles and perpetuate the invisibility of Aboriginal ways of knowing, doing, and being. Aboriginal leaders and educators may face challenges in advancing their careers within a system that does not fully embrace their leadership approaches. The expectations for conformity to Western leadership norms can hinder their progression.

Self Determination and Aboriginal Community Leadership

Self-determination and Aboriginal Community leadership are closely intertwined concepts that emphasise the rights, autonomy, and agency of Aboriginal Communities in shaping their own destinies and determining their future.

Self-determination and decolonisation are a key focus for Aboriginal teachers in leadership roles. Teachers actively support Community work and leadership and the development of children into healthy young adults within the Aboriginal Community – children who in turn will take up leadership roles and contribute to the self-determination of Aboriginal people. The emphasis on self-determination in leadership arises from personal experiences of trauma and the resilience demonstrated by Aboriginal middle leaders in overcoming it.

At the same time, Aboriginal middle leaders fight for recognition of the local Community leadership. Aboriginal Community leaders play a vital role in advocating for the rights, interests, and wellbeing of their Communities and their overall development. They represent their Communities in various forums, including government consultations, policy development processes, and negotiations with external stakeholders. They ensure that Aboriginal voices are heard, respected, and integrated into decision-making processes. Aboriginal middle leaders recognise the strengths of Community members, and because of their depth of insight, respect for Community, and facilitation skills, they make it possible for Community member involvement to benefit children's learning.

Culturally Responsive Leadership

Culturally responsive leadership ensures that educational transformation respects Aboriginal cultural identities and values, thereby leading to lasting and meaningful change. Culturally responsive leadership approaches leverage Aboriginal leaders' cultural competence to create safe and culturally sensitive spaces that lay the groundwork for transformative initiatives promoting equity and inclusivity.

The approach of Aboriginal middle leaders to governance is rooted in their Aboriginal worldview, particularly the notion that all things are connected in a web of relationships and the concomitant responsibility of care. As First Nations authors Ambelin and Blaze Kwaymullina explain:

> In Aboriginal philosophy the universe is a pattern comprised of other patterns, of systems inside systems. It is a holistic view in which everything is interrelated and interdependent. Nothing exists in isolation. All life – and everything is alive in an Aboriginal worldview – exists in relationship to everything else.
>
> (2010, p. 196)

Aboriginal knowledge systems are built on the foundation that all relationships are interconnected. This interconnectedness extends not only to human relationships but also to the relationships between humans and the natural world, the spiritual realm, and all aspects of existence. Interconnected relationships are fundamental to the way that knowledge is acquired and understood. Stemming from this worldview are several key values and concepts which

Aboriginal middle leaders work with every day (Graham, 2008; Kwaymullina & Kwaymullina, 2010): Aboriginal relationality views the school system as embedded in a web of interlinked relationships involving all the staff, children, families, and Communities served by the school. The relationship is not one-way. Schools are not just an education service provider to the broader Community. Schools play the role of an active participant, in a two-way, ongoing, respectful, and reciprocal relationship, where all parties possess rights, command respect, and have responsibility, obligations, and expectations of one another. Within this context, Aboriginal relationality emphasises the significance of instilling a sense of connection and shared responsibility within the education system. Integrating the principles of relationality into the education system represents a transformative step towards acknowledging and respecting Aboriginal laws, values, and worldviews. This relationship signifies the education system's commitment to moving away from a top-down, authoritative approach and embracing a more inclusive, collaborative model of engagement with all Communities. It places a strong emphasis on co-design with Elders, parents, and Community partnerships, recognising the importance of involving all stakeholders in shaping the educational landscape.

Leading in Practice

Culturally Responsive Leadership

Aboriginal middle leaders play a critical role in recognising and harnessing the strengths of their community members and Elders for the benefit of all children's learning. Middle leaders shared that they use their Aboriginal standpoint, insights, skills, and deep understanding of their community's culture, values, and traditions to foster meaningful Aboriginal community involvement in education (Tur et al., 2010). This high level of cultural competence allows them to appreciate the strengths and contributions of community members in a way that respects and honours their heritage in a culturally safe manner. As culturally responsive leaders, Aboriginal middle leaders bridge the gap between the formal education system and the community by effectively conveying information, needs, and goals in a culturally sensitive manner. The stories of middle leaders presented here challenge the conventional notion of leadership as tied to a specific role or title in an institution. Leadership can manifest in many ways, including through mentorship, support, and advocacy for the success of others.

Taylorism or Ecologies of Practices

Schools have embraced Taylorist, scientific management approaches to organising school and school leadership for decades. This approach focuses on efficiency, standardisation, and hierarchy that mirror the industrial processes of factory. Children sit in rows and teachers and leaders are organised and disciplined or even infantilised (Grice, 2025) within the organisation of the school.

With this model, middle leaders are simply central cogs in the wheel of efficient education, with neoliberal values. Leaders are not nurtured, and neither are students. This understanding of schooling is in stark contrast with ecological approaches to understanding the practices of schooling as living and human and evolving. Ecologies of practices (Kemmis, 2022) inter-relate with each other and co-influence each other. Ecologies are also about growth but with a focus on wellbeing, change, and flourishing. Leading with an ecological approach involves putting people and relationships first.

Tom Batty explains his identity in relation to leading Wildwood Forest School:

> I'm not a teacher. I'm a farmer. For a while now I've struggled with how to describe what I do. Particularly because anything like teacher or educator was too strong. It implied that my role was to take little blank canvasses and make them into something of my choosing using the information that I have that they currently don't have. Don't get me wrong. There is a place for teachers. But it's not me. What I do is much more like farming. I place children in an environment where they have the best possible resources to grow. I don't provide the growth. I can't. They do that themselves. In reality, I can only hinder or encourage the growth and it's all in the environment. Just like a seed needs the right soil, the right moisture, the right temperature, etc. A child needs to feel that they are safe, to feel comfortable to ask questions, to feel connected to peers, to feel free to be silly, to know that an adult believes in them, to know they will be listened to. Kids need the right environment first. Not the right information first. If we get that right, they flourish. So, I guess you can call me farmer Tom.

The educators working with Tom and the children at Wildwood Forest School also identified with the environment and the needs of children first and their educator identities as qualified early childhood educators second. They left environments where compliance overtook learning and placed the emotional and learning needs of children last, including in preschools where play was mandated for children and educators followed children for the purposes of recording their actions, not supporting their learning. Wildwood Forest School enabled the educators to *be* educators again.

Role Modelling

The senior and middle leaders in this chapter were role-modelling (Archard, 2012; Koh, Koh & Renganathan, 2023) how to create safe spaces for open dialogue in meetings, creating opportunities to lead together in practice. Their practices related to their values which then drove their purpose in leading together. They were aware of what practices they wanted to adopt as a leadership team, including modelling self-care and work design. They modelled motivation and engagement with others, demonstrating competence. They modelled interpersonal skills by being approachable, empathetic, honest, and actively communicated. They modelled reflection, communication, discussion, and feedback. Leaders made time for planning together and accepted that disagreement was part of the process of reaching consensus as they actively and authentically involved everyone. These practices were motivated by valuing everyone, including students, staff, and the wider school community, fostering learning.

Autonomy and Collective Agency

Leaders avoided *done to* practices wherever possible and focused on *done with* practices through genuine listening and action. They were committed to thinking and planning together, deciding, and acting upon feedback. This required a change to the material economic arrangements in their school, including meeting times, spaces, and places.

Autonomy-supportive practices based on SDT may include inviting participation, offering choice, active listening to build understanding of educator's perspectives, and providing clear links between tasks and their purpose. These practices can help to build internal motivation and engagement (Collie, 2023).

The framework for readiness to lead for middle leaders outlined in Chapter 1 (Day & Grice, 2019) invites leadership teams to consider the social norms, expectations, and practices that enable them to agree on joint work, connected expertise, and commitment to practice together: thinking, planning, deciding, and acting. Schools can know students and how they learn only through leading together. From this work, school leadership teams can carefully consider their shared values and purpose and pull together the practices that help leaders come together in solidarity and shared purpose.

Practicing Solidarity of Purpose

Leading with collective purpose depends on a deep knowing of people. Solidarity requires understandings not just of curriculum, policy, wellbeing, and students but of the intersubjective spaces between people where vision and values are lived in action. Habermas (1984) describes intersubjective places as the life worlds of people that exist beyond system worlds. Husserl (1936) notes that they are facilitated by the practices of empathy. Understanding intersubjective space builds solidarity as it involves sharing of power. Stetsenko (2013) names solidarity 'collectividual' responsibility as it is shared between people.

Solidarity that comes from collective responsibility has the capacity to transform leading in schools because schools are social spaces. Understanding social space is at the heart of the purposes of education and becomes what we value when we lead together. Solidarity requires justice, hospitality, commitment, courage, humility, curiosity, and a leap of faith (Hunt-Hendrix & Taylor, 2024). They suggest that if we instead choose to believe in other people, particularly during times of crisis, we can transform schools. The practice sections in our book enable these ideas in practice.

The practices of empathy build solidarity. Part of collective solidarity comes not from curriculum but from pedagogy, from the reciprocal nature of leading the child, so that they can go into the world. Tom Batty explains what self-directed adventure education is at Wildwood Forest School:

> I grew up in the 'trust and attention' paradigm of learning. It said, you must trust the curriculum because one day it will be relevant. It also said, because this curriculum is currently irrelevant, it is also boring. To combat such a challenge, it did one of two things. It either told me that I struggled with paying attention and would have so much potential if I only listened properly, or the on the flip side it sometimes made the boring curriculum capture my attention by coating it in stuff like kinesthetic and audio-visual teaching techniques, etc.
>
> I much preferred it when the teachers worked hard to make the boring stuff interesting. But as I look back on it, I now realise that it actually taught me a very clear message – the stuff I was meant to learn was not inherently interesting to every kid. Sure, some kids found parts of the curriculum interesting, and for certain parts of my schooling life I was in the zone – when the content matched my interests. But they rarely lined up.
>
> That was the old paradigm of learning. It's ok. But it has some very real problems. At Wildwood we operate under a different paradigm. I call it the 'Self Directed Adventure Education' paradigm of learning. It starts with the assumption that kids are curious. They don't need to 'be motivated to learn' or anything silly like that. They are humans. They cannot not learn. They want to make sense of the world around them. It's who we are. Therefore, we give the kids the space to 'Self Direct' the learning experience. If they are interested in something and want to explore it, then we follow their innate curiosity. But here is probably where we diverge most significantly from any normal school. We don't have a classroom. The 'learning' that they engage in doesn't really feel like 'classroom learning', mostly because it is not. We don't start with theory first and hope that one day it will be relevant. We start with the activity of their interest first and then we add the theory only afterwards, once it is relevant to the kid. But why 'Adventurous' activities? Well, really, it's just because they are usually much more fun than the stuff that happens in a classroom, that's all. And we like fun and don't really feel the need to defend it.

Solidarity is about putting children and curiosity first so that learning and wellbeing become integrally connected.

Practice Menu

Understanding leading as a practice can help you to understand how the practices of leading pedagogy, learning, and wellbeing leading can lead to solidarity of purpose and how leading together and understanding each other's perspectives and purpose can lead to growth and wellbeing. The practices of job crafting in the menu are a start to understanding your own role in leading with solidarity of purpose. Solidarity that sustains come from practices we explain below.

Current practices	*Questions about practice arrangements*	*Suggested practices for application*
Sayings (communication) Am I clear on what I want to say and do/more of/less of/differently? ***Doings*** What opportunities do I have to develop my capabilities? How much autonomy do I have? How do my actions and those of others relate with purpose? ***Relatings*** What opportunities do I have to develop my connections with others? Do I advocate for students/staff? What power do I have in my role? How do I use it? ***Dispositions (habitus)*** What motivates me? What are my levels of work engagement? Am I enjoying (engaged and motivated in) my leadership role? Am I clear on what holds me back?	***Cultural-discursive arrangements*** Am I clear on what my team wants to say and do more of/less of/differently? ***Material-economic arrangements*** Am I supporting my team in providing opportunities for autonomy, connection and competence? Do we use implementation planning to develop new habits in valued directions? ***Social-political arrangements*** What are the levels of engagement in my team like? Is our team motivated and enjoying work? Am I supporting my team to embed changes in habits? Do we advocate for students/each other? Power over or power with? How do we build solidarity together? ***Practice traditions*** Do I know what motivates my team? Am I clear on what holds my team back? How is what we do here connected with my role purpose, the roles of others? Is there collective shared purpose, vision, and action that brings solidarity? Who owns the school vision? Where is my part in it?	1. Culturally responsive leadership. Listen and demonstrate cultural humility. 2. Reconceptualise leading as part of ecologies of practices. Think about what leading practices or practice arrangements you can change from the middle leadership framework (Day & Grice, 2019) and beyond from your own context. 3. Role modelling interpersonal skills and reflection, and communication skills to reach consensus, authentically involving everyone. 4. Autonomy and collective agency through *done with* practices, through genuine listening action and commitment to thinking and planning together, and deciding and acting on feedback, using the framework. 5. Curiosity and learning are more than motivation, and deeply connects with autonomy. 6. Practicing solidarity of purpose is facilitated by empathy and a focus on the needs of children. It involves the practices of justice, hospitality, commitment, courage, humility, curiosity, and a leap of faith.

Summary of Key Points

- Educators need to be actively involved in authentic opportunities for wellbeing and learning in their daily work.
- Agency and engagement build motivation, which builds wellbeing.
- Self-Determination Theory is a framework for encouraging active participation in leading, by everyone.
- By tapping into the intrinsic motivation of students, teachers, and leaders and connecting work with purpose, leaders can foster autonomous motivation.
- Meeting the basic psychological needs of everyone for relatedness, competence, and autonomy enhances motivation for learning and improvement.
- Leadership teams need to consider their shared values and purpose and what social norms, expectations, and practices enable them to agree on joint work, connected expertise, and commitment to thinking, planning, deciding, and acting.
- Leaders build solidarity and with shared purpose through empathy and understandings of the spaces between us. Leaders need to consider the differences between 'done to' and 'done with' practices through genuine listening and action.
- Individuals need to consider their needs and purposes and how they align with collective purpose for students and colleagues.
- Schools and 'not schools' know students and how they learn by leading pedagogy reciprocally, together.

References

Apple, M.W. (1988). *Teachers and Texts: A Political Economy of Class and Gender Relations In Education*. New York: Routledge.

Apple, M.W., & Weis, L. (1983). Ideology and practice in schooling: A political and conceptual introduction. In M. Apple & L. Weis (Eds.), *Ideology and Practice in Schooling* (pp. 3–33). Philadelphia: Temple University Press.

Archard, N. (2012). Developing future women leaders: The importance of mentoring and role modelling in the girls' school context. *Mentoring & Tutoring: Partnership in Learning, 20*(4), 451–472. DOI:10.1080/13611267.2012.725980

Church, A.T., Katigbak, M.S., Locke, K.D., Zhang, H., Shen, J., de Jesús Vargas-Flores, J., Ibáñez-Reyes, J., Tanaka-Matsumi, J., Curtis, G.J., & Cabrera, H.F. (2013). Need satisfaction and well-being: Testing self-determination theory in eight cultures. *Journal of Cross-Cultural Psychology, 44*(4), 507–534.

Collie, R.J. (2023). Teachers' work motivation: Examining perceived leadership practices and salient outcomes. *Teaching and Teacher Education, 135*, 104348.

Day, C., & Grice, C. (2019). *Investigating the Influence and Impact of Leading from the Middle: A School-based Strategy for Middle Leaders in Schools*. The University of Sydney. https://hdl.handle.net/2123/19972

Deci, E.L., Olafsen, A.H., & Ryan, R.M. (2017). Self-determination theory in work organizations: The state of a science. *Annual Review of Organizational Psychology and Organizational Behavior, 4*(1), 19–43.

Giroux, H.A., & McLaren, P.L. (1992). Media hegemony: Towards a critical pedagogy of representation. In J. Schwoch, M. White, & S. Reilly (Eds.), *Media Knowledge: Readings in Popular Culture, Pedagogy, and Critical Citizenship* (pp. xv–xxxiv). New York: State University of New York Press.

Graham, M. (2008). Some thoughts about the philosophical underpinnings of Aboriginal worldviews. *Australian Humanities Review,* 45, 181–194. http://australianhumanitiesreview.org/2008/11/01/some-thoughts-about-the-philosophical-underpinnings-of-aboriginal-worldviews/

Grice, C. (2025). *The Practices of Leading Pedagogy.* Singapore: Springer.

Habermas, J. (1984). *The Theory of Communicative Action.* Boston: Beacon.

Hunt-Hendrix, L., & Taylor, A. (2024). *Solidarity: The Past, Present and Future of a World-Changing Idea.* New York: Pantheon Penguin Books.

Husserl, E. (1936/1970). *The Crisis of the European Sciences and Transcendental Phenomenology,* pp. 108–109. Translation by David Carr. Chicago: Northwestern University Press.

Ivory, W.M.F. (2009). Kunmanggur, legend and leadership a study of Indigenous leadership and succession focussing on the north west region of the Northern Territory of Australia, Student thesis: Doctor of Philosophy (PhD) - CDU, DOI:10.25913/5eb20d55e2c74

Jordan, R., & Leroy-Dyer, S. (2023). The leadership virtues of Aboriginal women in Australia. In T.P. Newstead & R.E. Riggio (Eds.), *Leadership and Virtues: Understanding and Practicing Good Leadership* (pp. 163–180). New York: Routledge.

Kemmis, S. (2022). *Transforming Practices: Changing the World with the Theory of Practice Architectures.* Singapore: Springer.

Koh, E.Y.H., Koh, K.K., & Renganathan, Y. et al. (2023). Role modelling in professional identity formation: A systematic scoping review. *BMC Medical Education 23*(1), 194. DOI:10.1186/s12909-023-04144-0

Korpershoek, H., Canrinus, E., Fokkens-Bruinsma, M., & De Boer, H. (2020). The relationships between school belonging and students' motivational, social-emotional, behavioural, and academic outcomes in secondary education: A meta-analytic review. *Research Papers in Education, 35*(6), 641–680.

Kubric, S. (2025). Millenial therapist @instragram accessed at https://www.sarakuburic.com/

Kwaymullina, A., & Kwaymullina, B. (2010). Learning to read the signs: Law in an Indigenous reality. *Journal of Australian Studies, 34*(2), 195–208. DOI:10.1080/14443051003721189

Magson, N.R., Craven, R.G., Ryan, R.M., Blacklock, F., Franklin, A., Mooney, J., Yeung, A.S., & Dillon, A. (2024). The associations between basic psychological need satisfaction at work and the wellbeing of Indigenous and non-Indigenous employees. *Transcultural Psychiatry, 61*(3), 440–456.

Morphy, F. (2007). The language of governance in a cross-cultural cultural context: What can and can't be translated. In L. Behrendt, J. Glanville, & N. Laing (Eds.), *Ngiya: Talk the Law – Volume 1. Governance in Indigenous Communities* (pp. 93–102). University of Technology Sydney.

Oscar, J. (2018). 'Because of her, we can'. *National Aboriginal and Torres Strait Islander Women's Conference.* Australian Human Rights Commission. https://humanrights.gov.au/about/news/speeches/because-her-we-can-national-aboriginal-and-torres-strait-islander-womens

Oxford University Press (n.d.). Motivation. In *Oxford English Dictionary*. Oxon: Oxford University Press. Retrieved 9 June 2025 from https://www.oed.com/dictionary/motivation_n?tab=factsheet#35683504

Ryan, R.M., Deci, E.L., Vansteenkiste, M., & Soenens, B. (2021). Building a science of motivated persons: Self-determination theory's empirical approach to human experience and the regulation of behavior. *Motivation Science*, 7(2), 97.

Ryan, R.M., Duineveld, J.J., Di Domenico, S.I., Ryan, W.S., Steward, B.A., & Bradshaw, E.L. (2022). We know this much is (meta-analytically) true: A meta-review of meta-analytic findings evaluating self-determination theory. *Psychological Bulletin*, 148(11–12), 813.

Sheldon, K.M., Abad, N., & Omoile, J. (2009). Testing self-determination theory via Nigerian and Indian adolescents. *International Journal of Behavioral Development*, 33(5), 451–459.

Slemp, G.R., Field, J.G., & Cho, A.S.H. (2020). A meta-analysis of autonomous and controlled forms of teacher motivation. *Journal of Vocational Behavior*, 121, 103459.

Slemp, G.R., Kern, M.L., Patrick, K.J., & Ryan, R.M. (2018). Leader autonomy support in the workplace: A meta-analytic review. *Motivation and Emotion*, 42(5), 706–724.

Stetsenko, A. (2013). The challenge of individuality in cultural-historical activity theory: "Collectividual" dialectics from a transformative activist stance. *Outlines: Critical Practice Studies*, 14(2), 7–28. https://www.outlines.dk/

Tur, S.U., Blanch, F.R., & Wilson, C. (2010). Developing a collaborative approach to standpoint in Indigenous Australian research. *The Australian Journal of Indigenous Education*, 39(S1), 58–67.

Van den Broeck, A., Ferris, D.L., Chang, C.-H., & Rosen, C.C. (2016). A review of self-determination theory's basic psychological needs at work. *Journal of Management*, 42(5), 1195–1229.

Yu, S., Chen, B., Levesque-Bristol, C., & Vansteenkiste, M. (2018). Chinese education examined via the lens of self-determination. *Educational Psychology Review*, 30, 177–214.

Zhou, S., Slemp, G.R., & Vella-Brodrick, D.A. (2024). Factors associated with teacher wellbeing: A meta-analysis. *Educational Psychology Review*, 36(2), 63. DOI:10.1007/s10648-024-09886-x

8 How Will We Get There?
Collective Job Crafting

Chapter 8 brings together all the ideas presented in this book so far and looks at how the practices from each chapter can come together in one continuous improvement process that we call 'collective job crafting'. Schools are dynamic places and change is constant. Practices influence other practices. Sustained processes are needed that support teachers and leaders to adapt to the constantly changing environments of schools over one-and-done approaches to leading initiatives. The five steps are outlined in this chapter. The steps and their processes have been expanded on in each previous chapter, and come together in Chapter 8. The steps themselves are explicit, but the processes or practices within each step are suggestive. Step 5 leads back to Step 1 in a continuing, sustainable process of intentional reflection, continuous improvement, and sustainability where there is no end point.

Rather than saying,

> "This is a new process we're putting in place, you guys now need to implement it within your teams", it became: "This is the challenge we've got. This process isn't working for us as a collective now. Let's work through it. What do we need to change?"

What is Collective Job Crafting?

Collective Job Crafting is different from individual job crafting. The former involves people working together to craft their jobs as part of a collective. Collective job crafting becomes the *us* work of working together to achieve a shared priority.

There is a lot of literature on the effectiveness of individual job crafting for role efficiency and productivity (Clinton et al., 2024; Tims & Bakker, 2010). Individuals craft their job on a regular basis, often with deep intentionality and as part of their daily practice through the everyday choices they make about their key priority for the day, through the creation of 'to do' lists, and even through procrastination (Berg et al., 2013; Alonso et al., 2019).

Collaborative job crafting (Wrzesniewski & Dutton, 2001; Llorente-Alonso & Topa, 2019) is a way of designing work with others in a team situation. It is a way of actively agreeing upon tasks together in accordance with people's needs and strengths. Collaborative job crafting might be planned. Sometimes, due to people's availability, others need to take on work tasks. On other occasions collaborative job crafting it may happen during busy situations on the fly. Collaborative job crafting is different from mandated delegation as it is negotiated in the moment, collectively, so that teams can function in their daily practices. It focuses on people working together. Llorente-Alonso and Topa (2018) found that the vigour, dedication, and absorption that individual job crafting creates can lead to collaborative job crafting and to improved job satisfaction and engagement.

Llorente-Alonso and Topa (2018) propose that the success of collaborative job crafting may be related to the level of interdependence within a team. The best way to know students and how they learn is to be an interdependent collective, an *us*. For this reason, we prefer the term '*collective* job crafting' because it encapsulates the shared nature of leading pedagogy through learning and wellbeing and our individual responsibilities to hone our craft, both individually as we teach and lead and as a collective, together. Collective job crafting is regular and intentional design of work through an agreed process, with agreed priorities for action. It is sustained through commitment to following the process and through action. This regular commitment to working together creates an approach that enables the individuals to identify not only as collaborators but as a collective, as *us*.

Collective job crafting is about excellence in optimal conditions and about moving from survival to thriving in suboptimal conditions. The diagram below outlines our collective job crafting process. The collective job crafting process can be utilised at team, department, or whole-school level or even by a whole school system (Figure 8.1).

Figure 8.1 Collective job crafting process.

Step 1 *(Who are we?)* draws on guidance from the Introduction and Chapter 1 from a clear understanding of the specific school context (including students), self-awareness, and purpose. Step 2 *(How do we work together?)* emerges from Chapters 3 and 4 where understanding each other's experiences, struggles, and strengths and gives guidance about how to work together. Step 3 *(What do we need?)* stems from Chapter 5 and involves identifying problems and practices that need to change. Step 4 *(How can we get there?)* draws on Chapter 6 and looks at the process of change in schools. Step 5 *(How are we going?)* is based on Chapter 7 and involves reflection on outcome and process and a return to shared purpose.

Examples from Schools

Paramount School is a school committed to its community. The large leadership team are professional and friendly. The principal builds relationships within the team by engaging with each leader individually during meetings. He gives space to confident leaders and sits with the quieter leaders to support their inclusion. The school is in a lower socioeconomic area, and it could be easy to assume that teaching and leading at Paramount are more difficult. The daily challenges bring solidarity among the leadership team where they solve complex learning and wellbeing issues together. Paramount's decision to participate in collective job crafting came from a place of strength rather than in response to crisis. When the leadership team considered '*Who are we?*' in **Step 1**, they reflected individually and collectively and agreed as a leadership team that in many ways they were already effective. As one leader shared:

> We were fairly effective before we started doing this, but we were asking, how can we move forward as a team together? It was understanding why – the importance of making changes, developing strategies and leadership potential.

The team knew their strengths and recognised the challenges in having everyone aligned with key priorities in their school and sharing who was going to lead them.

Prior to collective job crafting, the workload of middle leaders in this busy school made them feel defeated before they began:

> If we want to implement change, if you don't have buy-in from staff, then that's not going to happen. Is it lacking agency by choice? Because sometimes there's, 'oh there's too much on my plate I don't want to partake in that … I've got my plate so full that I don't have space for more.' I don't think that they see it as job crafting, it's more like, 'I'm just adding more to my plate, and I can't do that right now'. There's no agency there in that space.

Middle leaders push back on workload when initiatives don't come from them or the details of them aren't created by them. Agency is the capacity to genuinely lead an initiative. The senior leadership team at Paramount School had a challenge to support the leadership team to see that genuine leading together is about not adding to people's individual plates but rather sharing plates which have the potential to lessen what is on one person's plate. This led the leadership team to carefully consider Step 2.

For **Step 2** (*'How do we work together?'*), the senior leaders decided together that giving middle leaders the autonomy to lead meant that senior leaders needed to step back and trust them more. This was a complete change in their thinking and practice where they sought advice from middle leaders and let them make decisions rather than requesting that they implement initiatives driven by senior leadership. One senior leader comments:

> Rather than saying, 'This is a new process we're putting in place, you guys now need to implement it within your teams', it was very much about, 'This is the challenge we've got, this process isn't working for us as a collective. Now, let's work through it, what do we need to change?' It was providing the opportunity for middle leaders to have ownership of decision making in the school rather than feeling as though it was being imposed.

Middle leaders were strengthened by a consultative and trusting senior leadership team that knew how to let go and support middle leaders to make whole-school decisions, which enabled middle leaders to lead. This enabled the team to ask more clearly what they needed.

Paramount School knew that they needed space and time to develop their middle leaders. Sustained attempts to adapt to change are needed, and these take time to develop. There is often little time to ask, '*What do we need?*', and **Step 3** (*'What do we need?'*) invites this opportunity. One leader writes:

> Another barrier is creating that space and time to be able to take the time to actually shift things. That it is about the development of leadership.

They recognised the importance of Step 3 to enable the space for identifying needs. Rather than being reactionary and focusing on yet another change, Paramount knew that it needed to be proactive and focus on supporting its leaders over changes themselves. Focusing on middle leaders would give them the space to determine changes to curriculum, the new literacy strategy, and wellbeing initiatives in the school. The process was not smooth. There was initial resistance and lack of motivation and organisation from some middle leaders in this new way of working, and some middle leaders responded:

> We've never done it like that before, why would we change, why would we start doing this?

Breaking down the barriers to working collectively in Steps 2 and 3 meant involving middle leaders in **Step 4** ('How do we get there?'). Step 4 involved practical solutions. The key priority the school leadership team identified was to reduce the administrative burden of their leaders. Developing and discussing together were forms of improving as they worked out how to progress. They were positive about collective job crafting because they recognised that it was helping them to achieve their key priority:

> We are continually looking at ways to job-craft and ways to break down that administrative burden that was identified in our sessions as one of the key difficult elements of people's roles. I think we're very proactive. We're still looking at how we're using our time as leaders and are we getting the best possible results out of the time that we're providing. That has been an ongoing discussion this year. I aspire to be in the that improving phase, but I think we're very much developing. I think that's a healthy place to be right now.

The leadership team needed to build trust to work collectively. **Step 4** ('How do we get there?') involved trust-building. The collective job crafting process built trust:

> The most powerful thing that we did was having those strong processes: this is what we discussed, this is what your ideas were, this is what the next step is, this is the end result. People could see that regardless of whatever came up throughout it, that we were going to support decisions that were being made and that we were going to follow through with what the team set out to achieve.

When senior leaders demonstrated trust, it built trust in others. The most powerful message was that senior leaders recognised this change in their team from the process:

> The relationship [between leaders] is meant to be built on trust and that trust comes from the process. That's something that we were very mindful of as the senior executive were making sure that if we were going to open this dialogue and begin these conversations, then we need to really be strong in supporting and being consistent with how we follow up, and if we're going to ask for people to be involved, we need to just accept that even if it wasn't exactly the direction, we were going we have to put the trust in the work that people were doing and accept that this is what was going to happen as a result and really empower the team to make those decisions.

Step 4 invites leadership teams to focus beyond areas of interest into one agreed priority across the school to work on together, building consensus and reducing stress by reconceptualising their purpose as leaders together across the school, beyond siloed areas:

> The senior leadership team were working together trying to break down those walls of 'this is my role and my team', and who they supervised, looking broader. The language of leading beyond the middle really is what we can try to drive into the team. Middle leadership was not just about their areas. It was to support each other across the whole school.

Senior leaders recognised that the school would *get there* with the priority of communicating by working together, for the betterment of the school, and that leading together is about a school-wide focus. A senior leader explained their new way of working together:

> If I see an issue and I want to make some change, I'll bring it up with the group. And everyone in that group is very supportive and are happy to look at changing things, adapting things for the betterment of the school or for the betterment of students or teachers or community members.

Step 5: How are we going? Is a reflective process. As leaders went through the cycle of reflection, senior leaders identified that they needed to demonstrate significant commitment to giving the middle leadership team the time they needed to work collectively: *If we can buy a little love and a little bit more heart, there's intention. It's how to do that authentically.*

As the team reflected on their key priority, they started to consider how they could cut down on administrative burdens:

> Cross-faculty, how can we cut down on some of the administrative load that we have? Also, if we have a department teaching paragraph writing, why are we not collaborating as an entire cohort with middle leaders running a workshop as opposed to standalone isolated classrooms? We're looking at where things align and how to trim down and delegate to different faculties.

Having agreed upon their priority, senior leaders reflected on how their practices have changed, as they demonstrated their commitment to the autonomy of middle leaders by letting go and trusting them to deliver:

> We've been quite critical of ourselves, in the senior executive team, in how we were using and allocating our time with middle leaders. And this year we're taking a step back and we've said, your time is yours, you use it as you will. We've stopped putting parameters so much on the time that we're providing to them. We want them to have that little bit of creativity and time to dream ... not being so prescriptive in our expectations.

The collective job crafting process we have outlined through this scenario shows how leaders move from thinking about themselves as '*me*', through to what '*we*' can do as a collective, and then reflect on '*us*' and where to next.

Connecting Research and Practice

Throughout the book, we have recognised the importance of bringing '*me*' into your leadership and teaching role. We have talked about the importance of authenticity and bringing ourselves to work. Bringing the *me* parts to work are not separate from *we* or *us*; indeed, they do not exist without me. We are the sum of our parts, and the whole is different from the sum as Gestalt approaches demonstrate (Passons, 1975). What we build together, to form us as a collective, together, is new.

The *me* practices we have raised throughout the book include being self-aware, being authentic, using my pedagogical gifts, being motivated, learning, and taking ownership. There are practices within those practices that the book has uncovered.

When we work together, the '*we*' practices we have explored throughout the book that people do together include building external self-awareness, doing pedagogy, teaching and learning, leading, connected wellbeing, building trust and psychological safety, and demonstrating respect for others. Each of those practices also involves practices within them, but what is distinct about these '*we*' practices is that they always involve others. To have external self-awareness is to know how you come across with others. Pedagogy and teaching and learning inevitably involve more than one person, leading involves another, connected wellbeing is about those around you, and building trust and psychological safety is about others, as is respect.

Thinking about 'us' practices involves commitment to self and others that bridges 'me' and 'we', where individuals, together, become a collective and their shared practices become about

- Collective involvement (Chapter 1)
- Collective pedagogy (Chapter 2)
- Collective wellbeing (Chapter 3)
- Collective leading (Chapter 4)
- Collective responsibility (Chapter 5)
- Collective change (Chapter 6)
- Collective purpose (Chapter 7)

Leading together for pedagogy and wellbeing includes all these aspects as they come together in collective advocacy through the practices of empathy.

These are represented in the spiral found in the introductory chapter and as an ecology as outlined below (Figure 8.2).

Figure 8.2 Ecologies of practices for leading together.

The five steps in collective job crafting are a process of change and continuous improvement that involves collective communication, work, and reflection and negotiation about how to work together. It is a way of building an ecology of leading collectively in a school where the most important practice is empathy. Leading together is a trust-building process of consent and is aimed at increasing wellbeing and reducing stress. In this way, collective job crafting is a way of knowing how to manage change but choosing to do change rather than having change done to you. The scenario above has shown how collective job crafting can be done at the school level.

Social Network Theory

Social network theorists (Daly, 2010; Liu et al., 2017) map the support networks between people so that they can understand how people network and connect. It can be valuable to understand how leaders in schools connect with each other and the extent to which they do connect, and connect with senior leaders and other teachers, so that leadership in a school can be truly understood. The leadership dynamics can also be mapped to understand more about their practices (Cowhitt et al., 2023) and understand the integral connections between teachers and leaders. As part of the process of collective job crafting, leaders could map their growing and changing connections as they work more closely together.

Jon Eckert (2017) focuses on the importance of leading together for student learning outcomes. He encourages a collective approach to leading learning. He also is optimistic and focuses not on roles but on the work to be done to improve schools fearlessly. Eckert (2017) provides important insights into how to work with others, across a range of contexts, without prescription. Our ideas about collective job crafting are simple and are also not prescriptive.

Leading in Practice

Step 1: Who are We?

Step 1 is about context. It invites teams to ask, 'Who are we?' This involves thinking about, communicating about, and understanding both our school and our context and middle leadership roles, practices, and capabilities. The role of middle leaders is contextual, as mediating influences enable or constrain their capacity to lead. The following questions may help all school leaders take the first steps:

- *What is happening right now for us in my place of work?*
- *What are the most important things about our school right now that we need to keep in mind?*
- *What are the most important things about us as educators at the moment that we need to keep in mind?*
- *What are the most important things about our students that we need to keep in mind?*
- *What are the two or three main contextual factors that we need to keep in mind?*
- *What should be the key priority? What should be our key action(s) from that singular priority?*

These questions can be supported through idea generation, which can be done in any number of ways, including simple brainstorming strategies that involve everyone. For example, writing individual answers on sticky notes and posting them on a wall. Multi-voting can be used to determine the key priority (also known as the Nominal Group Technique) so that the team can narrow responses down to the top two or three. We recommend using a structured brainstorming procedure like the Charette Procedure (https://www.mindtools.com/awydne8/the-charette-procedure). This builds consensus.

The ability to have a clear understanding of your school context and the needs of different groups, alongside self-understanding, underpins readiness for collective job crafting. Chapters 1 and 2 outline exercises that can help teams to address these questions, including the lolly task, mural, metaphors task, and gifts. These tasks support relational crafting. Leaders spoke out about why Step 1 matters:

> Regular participation in school-wide decision making would help middle leaders feel more empowered.
>
> There is something about the culture of middle leaders that has been in a holding pattern at our school. When middle leaders have a voice, they have a sense of ownership, and they will take responsibility to make it happen.

Step 2: How do We Work Together?

Step 2 involves a mutual understanding of each other's experiences, struggles, and strengths to know how to work together. Chapters 3 and 4 are about working together and considering what motivates educators in their work. Alongside motivation, we need to consider the assumptions that underpin our practices where trust and psychological safety are foundational for working together. Both of these practices build collaboration through communication.

We recommend building communication by using research-informed approaches such as the middle leadership framework (Day & Grice, 2019) to diagnose the leadership team's readiness to work together. Chapters 3 and 4 also include active listening strategies that need to be coupled with responding through action. Psychological safety underpins all collective work. This comes through repeated opportunities to speak and to listen and to be given responsibility for work. Two case study schools share how they worked together:

> Trust is developed by acknowledging that a person can make decisions within their teams and that they feel like they are going to get the support from you in whatever decision it was.
>
> Trust comes from the process. If we're going to ask for people to be involved, we need to just accept that even if it wasn't exactly the direction, we were going to have to trust in the work that people were doing and accept that this is what was going to happen as a result and really empower the team to make those decisions. That was the most powerful thing that we did. People could see that regardless of whatever came up that we were going to support decisions that were being made and that we were going to follow through with what the team set out to achieve.

Step 3: What do We Need?

Step 3 involves identifying problems, practices that need to change, and desired directions. Two simple approaches that are covered in Chapters 4 and 5 that can be used to generate lists include:

- Circle of Voices is a useful approach to identify problems and key areas of focus. For example, our case study school identified administrative burden as draining the team, interdisciplinary collaboration that would be a challenge and energise the team, and social connection as a resource. This may draw out psychosocial hazards.
- Meeting protocols can also support educators to identify and communicate their needs clearly.

As our school example reflected on what they needed to change, they knew that they were burnt out. They employed realistic thinking about what they could do next.

> I think we're still looking at how we're using our time as leaders and are we getting the best possible results out of the time we're providing. And that's been an ongoing discussion.
> The process helped us develop an awareness of understanding of why the changes were important to develop the potential within and between our leaders.

Step 4: How can We Get There?

Step 4 looks at the process of change in schools and leadership practices that enable sustainable change so that leaders can reflect on how to support teams in using their skills to create positive change whilst ensuring that their wellbeing is maintained. Chapter 6 gives guidance on how to get there. Substantial research helps us understand how context can support motivation and engagement. Job Demands-Resources Theory (Wrzesniewski & Dutton, 2001) tells us that the balance between demands and resources is important. A mismatch leads to negative consequences, such as burnout, which in turn affects work performance. Self-Determination Theory (Deci & Ryan, 1985) helps us to understand that the quality of motivation is driven by context. Specifically, when leadership practices support the autonomy, competence, and relatedness needs of individual team members, their motivation is more sustainable over time. Autonomy supportive leadership practices can help teams to move forward with commitment, purpose, and interest. This means that leaders' sayings, doings, and relatings can influence change in their schools. Via inclusive practices that are structured to include all voices, the best ideas can be collected, and commitment to the process can occur.

Ideally, we include an appreciation of educators' work demands and the resources they have available to meet them while providing an environment where motivation can thrive. One way to do this is by focusing on the single most important thing for right now: *the* priority, not *a* priority. Step 4 is about choosing a priority and working out what needs to be done. Step 4 is achieved by the processes outlined in Steps 1, 2, and 3. One school explained how they decided to cut their professional learning and administration load for middle leaders by working across departments:

> How can we cut down on some of the administrivia load across departments? We're looking at our scope and sequences and asking how we can trim down and delegate aspects to different faculties to share instead of all faculties teaching the same skills.

This form of collective job crafting enabled middle leaders to work together and not repeat the same task many times across the school.

Step 5: How are We Going?

Step 5 involves reflecting on the processes in relation to shared purpose. In this step, leaders ask:

- What is our purpose?
- Why are we here?
- What do we value most? Is this reflected in our decision and action?
- What is our collective responsibility?

These questions are evaluative questions that connect with the values of the group. Step 5 leads back to Step 1 in a continuous, sustainable process of intentional reflection and action for continuous improvement. There is no end point.

Collective job crafting is a way of leading beyond the middle. It involves advocating for students and for team members. Advocacy is a practice. Advocacy is derived from the Greek *parakletos*, which means advocate, comforter, and helper. Advocacy is about more than speaking out. It is an action of empathy and relationship that comes from leading collectively.

Collective job crafting is a brave act of advocacy with practices that involve

- Listening to people you work with
- Identifying issues together to support finding their key priority
- Giving and sharing information about options for addressing priorities
- Helping others to present and express their views and wishes and to understand and defend their rights.

Advocacy comes from deep moral purpose and involves collective action.

Practice Menu

The practices of collective job crafting connect people together in teams, schools, and systems in an ecology. Practices are living, interdependent actions (Kemmis et al., 2012, 2014) and represent ways of leading and learning together. Just like in real ecologies, people adapt to changes over time, and because learning and wellbeing are about living people, we are always adapting, and we never arrive. The spiral in the introductory chapter encapsulated all the practices needed to be developed between people over time. The practices of collective job crafting look like this in practice:

Current practices	Questions about broader arrangements	Suggested practices for application
Sayings (communication) What do people say about working together? Who is silent?	*Cultural-discursive arrangements* How can we return to shared purpose? Am I/Are we adapting?	Each question is a communication step. Intentional reflection on outcome and process where each step requires communication, psychological safety, and trust. Sustainable practices enable continuous improvement Collectively job crafting in teams to balance demands and resources Do this continuously and creatively Advocate during challenges
Doings Step 2: How do we work together? Step 4: How can we get there? Do I understand what my job is?	*Material-economic arrangements* Step 3: What do we need? Do conditions change? Are demands and resources balanced in my role? In my team? What is inside and outside your control or influence?	
Relatings Step 1: Who are we? Step 5: How are we going?	*Social-political arrangements* What can you do first and with whom? What are our experiences, struggles and strengths? Are we collectively job crafting in my team?	
Dispositions (habitus) Step 1: Who am I? Who are we?	*Practice traditions* What is the context of our school? What are the problems and practices that need to change? What are the processes of change in our school?	

Summary of Key Points

- This chapter has outlined the practices in each chapter, bringing them together with a simple framework.
- We can work alone effectively, but we can't do it all.
- Collective job crafting is a series of actions that enable people to work together as part of an endless, sustainable process.
- It is an action that can be used moment to moment within smaller teams or revisited regularly in larger school teams. It could be about distributing role descriptions that are too big; it could be about a contextual issue like syllabus reform, introducing a pedagogical approach, administrative challenges, managing a critical incident, or managing a

staffing issue (illness/staff shortages/cover). It could be about working together or a behavioural issue in a year group, an academic need in a cohort, or a topical issue in a school community (complaints, issues of emails from parents, truanting, etc.), managing lunch time and co-curricular activities, or planning a special school event. We hope that this gives you many areas where working together with an agreed process can be applied with your team(s).
- As part of the process of collective job crafting, leaders could map their growing and changing connections as they job-craft together as a collective.

References

Alonso, C., Fernández-Salinero, S., & Topa, G. (2019). The impact of both individual and collaborative job crafting on Spanish teachers' well-being. *Education Sciences*, 9(74), 2–9.

Berg, J.M., Dutton, J.E., & Wrzesniewski, A. (2013). Job crafting and meaningful work. In B.J. Dik, Z.S. Byrne, & M.F. Steger (Eds.), *Purpose and Meaning in the Workplace* (pp. 81–104). Washington, DC: American Psychological Association.

Clinton, M.E., Bindl, U.K., Frasca, K.J., & Martinescu, E. (2024). Once a job crafter, always a job crafter? Investigating job crafting in organizations as a reciprocal self-concordant process across time. *Human Relations*, 78(1), 91–119. DOI:10.1177/00187267241228997

Cowhitt, T., Greany, T., & Downey, C. (2023). Storytelling with networks: Realizing the explanatory potential of network diagrams through the integration of qualitative data. *International Journal of Qualitative Methods*, 22. DOI:10.1177/16094069231189369 (Original work published 2023).

Daly, A. (2010). *Social Network Theory and Educational Change*. Cambridge, MA: Harvard Education Press.

Day, C. & Grice, C. (2019). *Investigating the Influence and Impact of Leading from the Middle: A School-based Strategy for Middle Leaders in Schools*. http://hdl.handle.net/2123/19972

Deci, E.L., & Ryan, R.M. (1985). *Intrinsic Motivation and Self-determination in Human Behavior*. New York: Plenum.

Eckert, J. (2017). *Leading Together: Teachers and Administrators Improving Student Learning Outcomes*. Thousand Oaks, CA: Corwin. DOI:10.4135/9781506380179

Kemmis, S., Edwards-Groves, C., Wilkinson, J., & Hardy, I. (2012). Ecologies of practices. In P. Hager, A. Lee, & A. Reich, (Eds), *Practice, Learning and Change. Professional and Practice-based Learning*, vol. 8. Dordrecht: Springer. DOI:10.1007/978-94-007-4774-6_3

Kemmis, S., Wilkinson, J., Edwards-Groves, C., Hardy, I., Grootenboer, P., & Bristol, L. (2014). Ecologies of practices. In *Changing Practices, Changing Education*. Singapore: Springer. DOI:10.1007/978-981-4560-47-4_3

Liu, W., Sidhu, A., Beacom, A.M., & Valente, T.W. (2017). Social network theory. In *The International Encyclopedia of Media Effects*. Hoboken, NJ: Wiley. DOI:10.1002/9781118783764.wbieme0092

Llorente-Alonso, M., & Topa, G. (2018). Prevention of occupational strain: Can psychological empowerment and organizational commitment decrease dissatisfaction and intention to quit? *Journal of Clinical Medicine*, 7(11), 450. https://doi.org/10.3390/jcm7110450

Llorente-Alonso, M., & Topa, G. (2019). Individual crafting, collaborative crafting, and job satisfaction: The mediator role of engagement. *Journal of Work and Organisational Psychology, 35*(3), 217–226.

Passons, W.R. (1975). *Gestalt Approaches in Counselling.* Boston: Thomson Learning.

Tims, M., & Bakker, A.B. (2010). Job crafting: Towards a new model of individual job redesign. *SA Journal of Industrial Psychology/SA Tydskrif virBedryfsielkunde, 36*(2), 1–9. DOI:10.4102/sajip.v36i2.841

Wrzesniewski A., & Dutton J.E. (2001). Crafting a job: Revisioning employees as active crafters of their work. *Academy of Management Review 26*(2), 179–201.

Index

Pages in *italics* refer to figures, pages in **bold** refer to tables, and pages in ***bold italic*** refer to boxes.

Aboriginal Community Leadership 112–113
Aboriginal leadership and leading 103, 106, 111, 114
Aboriginal pedagogies 107, 113
Action Research 12
active listening 55, **58**, *59*, 98, **100**, 131; listening 7, 11–12, 31–33, 42, 62, 67–69, 72–73, 74, *75*, 93, 112, 116, **118**
Addison, B. 38
agency 3, 5–7, 10, *11*, 13, 19, 23, 40, 63, *75*, 80, 94–95, 104–105, 112, *119*, 124–125; collective agency 103, 116, **118**
Ainscow, M. 96
Alexander, R. 40
Alonso, C. 122
Andrews, D. 83
APA Dictionary of Psychology 11
Apple, M.W. 111
Archard, N. 115
Armstrong, P. 82
arrangements 7, 12, 21, 37, 40, 86, 96; cultural discursive, material economic, social political 5, 12, **26–27**, 42, **58**, *75*, ***88***, **100**, 116, **118**, *134*
authentic 2–3, 7, 39, 41, 42, *43*, 63, 103, 116, **118**, *119*, 127–128
autonomous motivation 103, 109–111; motivation 3, 8, 15, 23, 50, 81, 84, ***88***, 95, 108, 116, *119*, 131–132
autonomy 10, *11*, 14, 23, 82, 86–87, ***88***, 96, 103, 105, 110–112, 116, **118**, *119*, 125, 132

Bakker, A.B. 50–51, **58**, 84, 122
basic psychological needs 110, *119*
Batty, T. 114, 117
Berg, J.M. 122
Bindle, U.K. 86
Blase, J. 83
Bono 92
Boyne, K. 37–39
Bransby, D.P. 67–69
Bristol, L. 12, 21, 83
Brookfield, S.D. 98
Brown, B. 71
Browning, P. 71
burnout 4, 7–8, 23, 31, 45–47, 49, 51–54, **58**, 72, 81–82, 86, ***88***, 132

Campbell, P. 96
capability 3, *11*, 92, 94, 96–97, **100**
Carden, J. 34
Carroll, A. 48
Chan, P.H.H. 85
Change 5, 7–8, 10, 12, 14, 16, 18, 21–22, 24, **26–27**, 31, 45, 62–63, 65, 72, 78–79, 87, ***88***, 122, 124–125, 128–129, 132, *134*; pedagogical change 5–6, 104
change champions 72, *75*
Chew, J.O.A. 83
Chirico, F. 49
Church, A.T. 109
Cilliers, P. 96
Clinton, M.E. 122
Coburn, C.E. 23
Collaborative for Academic, Social and Emotional Learning (CASEL) 46

collaboration 10, *11*, 18, 25, 56, 67, 72, 81, **88**, 92, 94, 96–98, **100**, 105, 131
collective 2–3, 6, 10, 14, 16, 21, 24, **27**, 38, 47, 89, 92, 96–97, 104, 116, 128
collective job crafting 122–124, 126, 128–129, 133, *134*; *collective job crafting process* 123
Collie, R.J. 48, 111, 116
Collins, J. 22
communication 4, 7, 14, 24, 56, 65, 68, 71, *75*, 93, 116, **118**, 131, *134*
communicative learning spaces 73
community 1, 6–7, 19, 46, 82, 106, 112–114
Conway, J.M. 83, 97
Costantini, A. 86–87
Courtney, S.J. 22
Cowhitt, T. 129
critical education praxis *see* praxis
Crowther, F. 37–39
culturally responsive leadership 113–114, **118**

Daly, A. 129
Datnow, A. 96
Day, C. 19–20, 25, **26**, 70–71, 82, 116, 131
de Lisser, R. 8
De Vries, J.D. 84
Deci, E.L. 46, 109–110, 132
democratic 3, 6, 71, 73, 104
Diamond, J. 40–41
Dutton, J. E. 86–87, 123, 132
Durlak, J.A. 46

Eckert, J. 129
Ecologies of Practices 5, 12, 114–115, *129*
Edmondson, A. 67–69, 73
Educational leadership 1, 7, 13, 15, 78
Edwards-Groves, C. 12, 21, 70–71, 83
Ehrich, L. 83
empathy 11, 31, 41, 42, 92, 116–117, **118**, *119*, 133
engagement *see* work engagement
English, F. 83
evaluation 5–6, 23–24, 28, 104
Evers, C. 81

Farrell, C.C. 23
Fink, D. 70–71
Fitzgerald, T. 71
Fleming, W.J. 54

Forssten Seiser, A. 13, 21, 37, 39, 72
Fox, K. 38
Francisco S. 13, 73
Fraser, P. 49
Freire, P. 61, 71
Fullan, M. 96

Gaines, K.A. 73
Ghamrawi, N. 47
gifts *see* pedagogical gifts
Giroux, H.A. 111
Goldshaft, B. 41, 73
Graham, M. 114
Grice, C. 13, 19–21, 25, **26**, 39–41, 70–72, 82–84, 95, 114, 116, 131
Gronn, P. 82
Grootenboer, P. 12, 21, 37, 70, 82–83
Guattari, F. 71
Gunter, H.M. 22
Gurr, D. 81

Habermas, J. 116
habits 1, 10, 13, 24, 26, **88**, **100**, **118**
Hall, D. 82
Hallam, K.T. 8
Hardy, I. 12, 21, 83
Hargreaves, A. 96
Harris, A. 82
Hascher, T. 48
Heffernan, A. 39
Hennerman, E. 96
Henrick, E.C. 24
Hickey, A. 40
hope 9, 12, 21, 38, 40, 41, 67, 107, 117
Hu, J. 67
Hunt-Hendrix, L. 117
Husserl, E. 116
Huta, V. 46

identity 3, 18, 37, 73, 107, 115
initiatives 4, 17, 19, 23, 82, 98–99, 113, 125
Innovative Designs for Enhancing Achievements in Schools (IDEAS) 83
instruction 3, 6, 39, 41, 67, 84, 104
International Classification of Diseases (ICD-11), World Health Organisation 52
interventions 4, 45, 54, **58**, 73
Ivory, W.M.F. 111

job crafting 7, 12, 24–25, 78–80, 84, 86–87, **88**, 89, 122

Job Demands-Resources model (JDR) 50, 86–87, *88*, 132
John-Steiner, V. 96
Jordan, R. 112

Kant, I. 71
Kassandrinou, M. 67
Keddie, A. 21
Keij, D. 70
Kemmis, S. 12, 21, 37, 83, 114, 133
Koh, E.Y.H 115
Kolb, A. 98
Korpershoek, H. 110
Kotter, J.P. 72
Kross, E. 34
Kubric, S. 103
Kwaymullina, A. 113–114

Lakomski, G 81
Langalotz, L 73
leading (pedagogy, learning) 1–11, 14, 16, 18, 21–23, 25, **26–27**, 28, 30, 32–33, 37–40, 54, 63, 80–83, 92, 130
leading together 1–2, 5, 9, 14, 17, 19, **26**, 27, 92, 125, *129*
Leithwood, K. 81
Leroy-Dyer, S. 112
Lewin, K. 12
lifelong learning 5–6, 104
Liu, L.B. 47, 129
Llorente-Alonso, M. 123
London, M. 34
Longmuir, F. 21, 39, 48
Lortie, D. 38

MacMahon, J. 54
Madigan, D.J. 51
Magson, N.R. 109
Mahon K. 12
Mansfield, K. 30
Maricuțoiu, L. 46
McCallum, F. 48
McCulla, N. 70–71
McKay, A. 39
me 2–3, 5–6, 79, 128
meetings 12, **26**, 31, 33, 35, 62, 68, 81, 87, 94–95, 105; meeting protocols 74, *75*, 98, **100**, 101, 131
mental health *see* poor physical and mental health
metaphor 22, 25, **26–27**, 62–63, 82, 130

middle leader 2, 4–5, 8–9, 17–20, 22–23, 25, **26–27**, 31–32, 38, 62–63, 69, 79–80, 82, 92–94, **100**, 105, 113, 125–127, 130
middle leadership framework *20*, 25
Mishra, A.K. 72
motivation *see* autonomous motivation
Morphy, F. 112
Murphy, C. 54
Murry, J.M. 30

Neenan, M. 99

OECD (Organisation for Economic Co-operation and Development) 7, 49
Oscar, J. 112
O'Neill, O. 71
Ormiston, H.E. 51

Pajalic, A. 53
Palmer, P.J. 37
Parker, S.K. 86
Passons, W.R. 128
pedagogical approaches 2–3, 32
pedagogical gifts 3, 30, 37–39, 42, 128; gifts 14–15, 22, 32–33, 40, 42, 130
pedagogy 1–3, 6, 10–11, 13–14, 21, 30–32, 37–41, 42, *43*, 79, 83, 104, 123, 128
Pedagogy and wellbeing spiral 1, 11
Penuel, W.R. 23–24
performance 4, 6, 34, 36, 50, 61, 67–70, 109, 132
Pietarinen, J. 86
poor physical and mental health 4, 35, 46, 49–51, 53, **58**
Postman, N. 71
practices 1, 3–5, 9–12, 19, 21, 25, 39–40, 83, 96, 104, 106, 108, 111, 116
Practice Menu **26**, 41, **58**, 74, 78, 87, **100**, **118**, 133
praxis 12–13, 22, 83
Preskill, S. 98
priority 1, 5–7, 12, 16, 22, 31, 50, 79–80, 85, 104, 122, 124, 126–127, 130, 132, 133
professional 4, 38, 41, 52, 70; professional capital 96
professional development 50, 95
professional learning 2, 7–9, 23–24, 65, 81–82, 87, *88*, 97, 99, 105, 132

psychology 2, 9, 11, 34, 45; organisational psychology 1, 14
psychological safety 8, 10, 14, 23, 46, 61, 64–65, 67–69, 71–74, 80, 128, 131
psychosocial hazards, risks 4, 49–51, **58**, 70, 85
purpose 1, 4, 6, 8, 10, 12–13, 17, 22, 24, **26–27**, 30, 39, *43*, 65, 78, 84, 92, 96, 103, 115–116, **118**, *119*, 128, 133

reciprocal 7, 21, 23, 61, 71, 83, 112, 114, 117, *119*; reciprocity 4
recovery 53, 78, 84–85, *88*
reflection 1–2, 7, 14, 24, 34, 63, 66, 97, 116, 122, 124, 127, 129, *134*; critical self-reflection 10, *11*, 42, 107
Research-Practice Partnerships 19, 23–25, 28
research 4, 8–9, 12, 19, 24, 28, 45–49, 51, 54, 67–68, 70–71, 79–80, 84, 86, 96, 103, 108–109, 128, 132
respect 4–5, 14, 19, 22, 31, 38, 40, 48, 62, 70, 74, *75*, 82, 96, 98, 107, 113–114, 128
responsibility 5, 14, 16, 22, 39, 41, 62, 78, 80, 82, 93, 106, 113–114, 116, 128, 130–131, 133
Riddle, S. 40
Riordan, G. 99
Roberts, A. 25–26, 78, 81
role titles, position, descriptions 1, 5–6, 16, 21–22, 27, 31–32, 37–38, *43*, 50, 79, 130
Rugulies, R. 54
Ryan R.M. 46, 109–110, 132

Schaufeli, W. **58**
Schecter, C. 97
Schulte, P.A. 49, 51
self-awareness 5, 30, 34, 41, *43*
Self-Determination Theory 103, 109–110, *119*, 132
Shaked, H. 97
Sheldon, K.M. 109
Silapurem, L. 86
Sjølie, E. 73
Slemp, G.R. 110–111
Smith, T. 12
Social Network Theory 129
Socratic questioning 99
solidarity 5, 10, 12, 66, 74, 103–104, 116–117, **118**, 124

Sonnetag, S. 84
Spillane, J.P. 22, 81
Stetsenko, A. 116
Stiegler, B. 71
Sugrue, E.P 51
Sutton, J. 99

Taylor, A. 117
Taylorism 114
teaching techniques 2–3, 39
The theory of practice architectures 21, 83
Tims, M. 86–87, 122
together 4–6, 11–12, 15–16, 19, 23–24, 37, 40, 61, 72, 78–80, 92, 96, 101, 106, 116, 122, 131, 133, 135
Topa, G. 123
trust 5, 10–11, 14, 17, 19, 24, 31, 61–66, 70–71, *75*, 112, 126, 129, 131
Tuerktorun, Y.Z. 85
Tur, S.U. 114

us 2–6, 18, **26**, 37, 122–123, 128, 130

values 1–3, 5, 7, 10, 13, 16, 22, 39, *43*, 70, *75*, 79–80, 83, 94, 106, 109, 114, 116, *119*
Van den Broeck, A. 50–51, 109–110
van Manen, M. 39–41, 97
Viac, C. 49
vision 5, 7, 13, 16–17, 32, 80–81, 93, 104, 106, **118**
voice 6, 11, 19, *59*, 61, 67, 73, 93, 104, 106, 130, 132; circle of voices *75*, 98, **100**, 131

Waber, J. 48–49
Walker, A. 99
Walsh, L. 21
Wasserman, S. 98
we 2–3, 5, 9, **26–27**, 38, 41, 42, *75*, 78, *88*, 96, **100**, **118**, *123*, 124–125, 128, 130–133, *134*
Welsh, R.O. 24
wellbeing, leading wellbeing 1–7, 9–14, 16, 21, 23, 30, 32, 38–39, 42, 45–49, 51, 54, **58**, *59*, 70, 79–80, 87, 103, 110, 128
Wenger, E. 82, 96
whole child, whole educator, whole school, whole self 1–5, 10, 13, 22, 41, 72, 79, 98, 104–105, 123, 128
Wilkinson, J. 12, 21, 37, 39, 72, 83
Woods, P.A. 25–26, 78, 81

work engagement 10, 46, 48, 51, 53, 57, **58**; engagement 7–8, 15, 80, 85, 111, 114, 116, **118**, 123; Utrecht Work Engagement Scale **58**
workload 7, 16, 19, 22, 28, 48, 66, 78, 89, 107, 124–125
The World Health Organisation 52–53
Wrzesniewski, A. 86–87, 123, 132

Youngs, H. 82
Yu, S. 109

Zeng, G. 39
Zhang, F. 86
Zhou, S. 48, 110

For Product Safety Concerns and Information please contact our EU representative GPSR@taylorandfrancis.com Taylor & Francis Verlag GmbH, Kaufingerstraße 24, 80331 München, Germany

Printed and bound by CPI Group (UK) Ltd, Croydon, CR0 4YY
31/10/2025
01989109-0002